LIAR'S KINGDOM

LIAR'S KINGDOM

How to Stop Trump's Deceit and Save Democracy

ANDREW WEISSMANN

First published in the USA in 2026 by Little, Brown and Company
An imprint of Hachette Book Group
1290 Avenue of the Americas, New York, NY 10104
littlebrown.com

First published in the UK in 2026 by Headline Press
An imprint of Headline Publishing Group Limited

1

Cataloguing in Publication Data is available from the British Library

Hardback ISBN 978 1 0354 4724 4
Trade Paperback ISBN 978 1 0354 4743 5

Offset in 12.6/18.1pt Minion Pro by Six Red Marbles UK, Thetford, Norfolk

Printed and bound in Great Britain by Clays Ltd, Elcograf S.p.A.

Headline's policy is to use papers that are natural, renewable and recyclable products and made from wood grown in well-managed forests and other controlled sources. The logging and manufacturing processes are expected to conform to the environmental regulations of the country of origin.

Headline Publishing Group Limited
An Hachette UK Company
Carmelite House
50 Victoria Embankment
London EC4Y 0DZ

The authorised representative in the EEA is Hachette Ireland,
8 Castlecourt Centre, Dublin 15, D15 XTP3, Ireland (email: info@hbgi.ie)

www.headline.co.uk
www.hachette.co.uk

To Lisa

The result of a consistent and total substitution of lies for factual truth is not that the lies will now be accepted as truth, and the truth be defamed as lies, but that the sense by which we take our bearings in the real world — and the category of truth vs. falsehood is among the mental means to this end — is being destroyed.

— Hannah Arendt

CONTENTS

LIAR'S KINGDOM

INTRODUCTION

It was spring of 2019, halfway through the first administration of Donald J. Trump, when I bounded breathlessly into my parents' favorite Manhattan restaurant. They had lunch here at the same table every Saturday afternoon, and today I was joining them — but as so often happened those days, I'd been running late. I had only recently returned to New York City from my latest stint in Washington, DC, where I'd just finished working as a senior prosecutor for Special Counsel Robert S. Mueller. I was still reorienting myself to both civilian life and the pace of the Big Apple.

My parents knew from my decades of work at the Department of Justice that, although we had a lot of catching up to do, it was going to be a pretty one-sided affair. As a government employee, I had learned to stay tight-lipped about my work. As they were both talkers, I knew this would not result in awkward silences. Sure enough, they delved headlong into what was happening to our country.

My father was a research scientist and my mother a Freudian psychologist. Between their two professions, they had a lot to say about our president and the current American political landscape. True to his training, Dad railed about the lack of data to support Trump's various pronouncements — a gap so pronounced that he concluded Trump was not just factually wrong, but intentionally so. Mom was focused more on the "why" question — why were so many people ready to accept such representations as true, when they were plainly false. "Cognitive dissonance" and "denial" were two concepts she expounded on.

I had given a lot of thought to these same questions. It was impossible not to, having just emerged from an investigation into Russia's incontrovertible interference in the 2016 election, which the president nonetheless frequently derided as "the Russia hoax." But on this day, I was less interested in sharing my own impressions with my parents than I was in getting theirs.

My parents had both been fresh out of college during the 1950s Red Scare, in which Senator Joseph McCarthy engaged in a hunt for communists who, he claimed, were infiltrating the government, the media, and universities. How, I asked, did that period compare to the time we were living in now? We had survived McCarthyism, and I probably was hoping they would reassure me that we'd survive this, too — that what we were experiencing was just another pendulum swing, one that would correct itself with time.

My parents were of one mind on my inquiry: the McCarthy era was worse. No doubt, they observed, Trump and McCarthy both resorted to lies and fabricated boogeymen as a means to gain and cling to power. My parents acknowledged that Trump, unlike McCarthy, had far more actual power than the senator to carry out his threats. But what made the demagoguery of the 1950s so scary, they said, was how alone you felt; no one was speaking out. People were too afraid. You felt completely isolated and unsupported. By contrast, although half the country may have supported Trump at the time of our lunch, the other half did not and was unafraid to say so.

Not one to view the world through rose-colored glasses, my father said that I was ignoring a more apt historical analogue: Germany in the 1930s. The same resort to lies and boogeymen; the same appeals to nationalism, victimization, and class warfare; the same misguided belief by the elites that they would be able to control the candidate when he came to power. My father had a more intimate awareness of this history than books alone could afford: he was born in Vienna, Austria, in 1930 and was Jewish. He and his parents managed to get out after the *Anschluss* in 1938, when the Germans marched into Austria and its borders were closed.

Dad rarely made comparisons to those times. It was understood in our family that they simply were not analogous to anything before or since. As he spoke, I found myself wondering, *Is Dad overreacting?*

I never got to tell him that he was all too right. My father died just before the COVID-19 pandemic, and today my mother suffers from acute dementia. It is one of God's small blessings that they are unable to compare the current American upheaval with what my father lived through as a boy in Europe. If they could, I know in my heart that their answer to my question would be quite different, given the brazenness of Trump and his enablers during his second presidency, and given the cowardly silence brought on by multiple acts of retribution. Neither do I have any doubt that Dad would continue to draw a historical parallel to prewar Germany. Although years have passed since our Saturday lunch conversation, it came flooding back when Senator JD Vance himself labeled Trump "America's Hitler" (which he later would retract). Now we are confronted daily with another analogy: Trump as a king, with unchecked power despite a system that is based on checks and balances to diffuse that power. This abuse of his position is noted by judges called on to adjudicate the excesses of his actions, as well as by millions of people across the globe in "No Kings" rallies protesting the exercise of power by this American president.

The questions that we discussed that afternoon at lunch remain particularly salient. How are we to deal with the core challenges to democracy we are confronting anew today — especially the fact that the truth no longer seems to matter and that our politicians lie with abandon, and without legal and political consequence? What does it mean for the longevity of a society when we no longer have a common ground?

I was still wrestling with these questions one day in the summer of 2025 as I walked from my digs on the Left Bank of Paris to my temporary NYU-France office, where I had begun drafting this book during time off from my "day job" teaching national security and criminal procedure courses at New York University School of Law. Each morning, I walked across the short bridge that connects two islands floating in the Seine — the tiny island of Île de la Cité and the even smaller Île Saint-Louis. From this vantage point I was confronted with two seemingly disparate monuments that, on this day, resonated with special force.

The first monument was the Mémorial des Martyrs de la Déportation, which commemorates those who died in the concentration camps established by the German Nazi Party. It comprises a series of subterranean concrete warrens, graphically recounting the horrors and cruelty of the deadliest of authoritarian regimes. The exhibit depicts a government with no functioning checks or balances — no independent news media or legal system to reveal and stop the crimes transpiring in the name of the German people. Walking through the memorial's windowless room after windowless room evokes by design that bygone system's oppression and persecution. No wonder that, many years later, FBI Director Louis Freeh required all incoming FBI special agents to visit the Holocaust Museum in Washington, DC, to understand the great power they soon would be privileged to wield and to absorb what can happen when that power goes unchecked.

The second monument before me that day was one of the great cathedrals of the Western world, Notre-Dame de Paris. Building began in the twelfth century, an astounding thousand years ago, but in 2019 it was engulfed in a ravaging fire that ignited in the wooden "forest" supporting its metal roof. Images of its charred beams, collapsed roof and spire, and the exposed ribs of its famed flying buttresses rocketed across the Internet, to our collective disbelief. I had taken the cathedral's permanence for granted, only to watch the sight of it vanish in thick smoke.

The reaction to Notre-Dame's devastation was immediate and uplifting: an outpouring within France and across the globe to support rebuilding the edifice. Architects, craftspeople, environmentalists, safety specialists, and preservationists were assembled. This team of specialists made critical decisions about how to rebuild, tempering the goals of historical accuracy in design and materials with the imperative of adding modern fortifications that would thwart another conflagration. Sprinkler systems, fire-retardant wood, and modern alert systems were all added to the project, even as the cathedral's original types of oak and limestone were reused as the primary construction materials.

These two disparate monuments, I realized, exemplify the main theme of this book: First, not to look away from the authoritarianism engulfing the United States. Second, to prepare for a time when we will be able to rebuild — but wisely. Like the choices made by the stalwart Notre-Dame team, we should not resort to a mere facsimile of what was there before the fire. We must incorporate new, sturdier elements in a design that respects the original but fortifies it for the future.

You may be wondering how on God's green earth I could have such dour thoughts instead of succumbing to the mesmerizing beauty of Paris, the most romantic of cities and a seemingly perfect antidote to the political turmoil back home. I was living, after all, that old joke: "What are the four best things about being an academic?" Answer: May, June, July, and August.

But my other "day job" keeps me tethered to the sobering daily churn of events in the United States, no matter where I may find myself on the globe. I am a legal analyst for the freshly rebranded MS NOW, as well as a co-host of an MS NOW podcast. The latter is entitled *Main Justice*, the nickname for the headquarters of the Department of Justice in Washington, DC. In a sign of where things stand, until January 2025 the podcast had been called *Prosecuting Donald Trump* and we kept tabs on the legal ins and outs of the four criminal cases against Donald Trump. With his inauguration and the dismissal of the two federal and one Georgia criminal cases against him, and the guilty verdicts in the New York state trial now on appeal, our podcast's old title was no longer an option. Neither was ignoring the daily blitzkrieg of news from America.

Witnessing the chipping-away at the rule of law is profoundly upsetting to many, of course. It certainly has been for me, having devoted my entire professional life to the legal system as, variously, a criminal prosecutor, a defense lawyer, and a teacher for over thirty years, including a stint as the general counsel of the FBI under Director Robert Mueller.

The developments hit me on a particularly personal level, as I have been the subject of not one but two Trump executive orders. The first one, in spring 2025, announced the revocation of the security clearances of a slew of perceived Trump enemies. Without any facts advanced to support the actions, Trump directed that I be stripped of my clearance. With this executive order, at least, I was in very good — and far more exalted — company, including the likes of Hillary Clinton, Joe Biden, Kamala Harris, and Liz Cheney. (A side note to the reader: When Tulsi Gabbard, the head of the intelligence community, carried out Trump's directive, she tweeted that she was revoking the clearance of "Andrew Weissman" — misspelling my last name. Whoever that fellow is, I am sorry to be the cause of his clearance being stripped. Oh, and one more side note: Having been out of government since 2019, I no longer held a security clearance, so the entire exercise was a performative show of retribution.)

The second executive order was more targeted. I was singled out in one of four executive orders targeting law firms, ostensibly because of actions that Trump found "detrimental to critical American interests." That is to say — as a court would later conclude in striking down the executive order as violative of the First Amendment — the law firms took on clients and positions with which Trump disagreed, such as representing asylum seekers and transgender clients.

The executive order against Jenner & Block accused the law firm of something else: having rehired as a partner "the unethical Andrew Weissmann" after I worked on the Special Counsel Mueller investigation. The executive order noted that I had returned to Jenner & Block after my "time engaging in partisan prosecution as part of Robert Mueller's entirely unjustified investigation." The executive order went on to say that the "numerous reports" of my "dishonesty" served to tarnish Jenner & Block, and was an "indictment" of its values and priorities.

In case the point wasn't clear enough, in his oral announcement of the executive order Trump called me a "bad guy," which seemed like a mild upgrade from his speech at the Department of Justice weeks earlier in which he used the salacious but unedifying noun *scum* to describe me. Stephen Miller, no doubt sensing his boss's mood, ranted on *Fox News* that I was a "moron" and "degenerate" (the latter term eerily invoking for me the identical language Nazis used to describe enemies of *that* state).

Although this time the Trump administration had managed to spell my name correctly, the executive order made a larger gaffe. It suggested that I still worked at Jenner & Block after leaving the Mueller investigation. In fact, I had left in 2021, four years before the 2025 executive order, something either Google or ChatGPT would have been able to quickly divine.

None of this was lost on federal District Judge John Bates, a Republican appointee who was hearing Jenner & Block's constitutional challenge to the executive order. He concluded that "it is evidently Weissmann's criticisms of the President and participation in a legitimate investigation of election interference that drew presidential disdain." Drawing the only conclusion possible if you still believe in facts and law, the court held that my "activity falls easily within the First Amendment's muscular protection for 'criticism of government and public officials.'" And with that, he declared the entirety of the executive order "null and void."

But the damage from this and other executive orders against law firms, academic institutions, and others is done. Some capitulated, some fought, and many were cowed into submission. Rather than find themselves on a governmental enemies list, they stay silent or complicit, as in the McCarthy era. They settle bogus lawsuits brought by Trump and his allies. They cede the defense of academic freedom to avoid losing critical scientific grants. They decline to bring good-faith litigation against administration policies so as not to become a target of illegal government retribution.

I did not escape the effects of such submissiveness. In spite of Judge Bates's ruling, law firms that were representing me quietly decided to withdraw. The publishing house that was first slated to release this book backed out within hours of Trump's executive order about Jenner & Block — proof that fear works, though not entirely: fearless editors and lawyers stepped into the breach, for me and many others.

The drama over the executive orders was transpiring at the same time that I was strolling through the charmed streets of Paris, which looked at every turn like a stage set from *La*

Bohème. But I was immune — at least on this occasion — to the city's siren song. And I am not the only expat who can say that.

Another example, one particularly dear to me, is the philosopher Karl Popper, an Austrian Jew who fled to Paris in the 1930s as it fell under Nazi influence. Popper's life's trajectory has personal resonance, given my own father's Austrian heritage and forced exile. I have since reclaimed my Austrian citizenship, something my father might have found deeply disturbing, but understandable given our current political predicament. In the span of a single generation, a father's flight from Europe and a son's return.

But Karl Popper is a source of inspiration for another reason, too. After leaving Austria, he penned his most well-remembered book, *The Open Society and its Enemies*, in which he extolled liberal democracy against the seductive ideologies of authoritarianism then sweeping influential segments of Europe. The antidotes to such "closed" societies, he argued, are democratic institutions, open and critical discourse, and the promotion of reason, pluralism, and the dignity of the individual. He believed that institutions and knowledge are fallible, and therefore must be open to reasoned debate based on evidence.

We would do well to heed Popper today, as we see the pernicious effects of the breakdown of these very same systems all around us. We see the demise of reasoned debate, the kind based on facts and not invective.

In searching for answers, I am unlike my parents — the scientist and the psychologist. I'm at core a lawyer and an institutionalist, so my focus isn't on why my fellow Americans are prepared to swallow Trump's lies whole. It's how our legal structures may be able to protect us from those lies going forward.

Today in the United States of America, a politician can blatantly lie to the electorate and suffer no legal consequence. This is in stark contrast to how we treat lies in innumerable other, less egregious circumstances than that of a politician who tells lies that fundamentally undermine a democracy. One feature of our judicial system is that it's had a singular aversion to dealing with the political lie. The lie is largely left to battle it out with the truth in some imagined "marketplace of ideas" — a system that, in practice, has not worked well to separate fact from fiction.

A "marketplace" metaphor, whatever its utility elsewhere, is particularly inapt for deciding factual issues. A marketplace may be a fine forum for subjective beliefs and ideas to compete against each other for acceptance by the general public, but it has no place in deciding incontrovertible or provable facts. Is gravity to be subject to a vote? Will the next cure for polio be decided by polling? Do facts have to duke it out with lies in a marketplace of ideas, in a Darwinian survival of the fittest? The "marketplace of ideas" metaphor, if it's even still applicable at all in this era of balkanized media, is not a useful way of thinking about cold, hard facts and incontrovertible lies.

With Karl Popper's vision of an "open society" front of mind, and with sights of the craftspeople reconstructing Notre-Dame as my daily example, I have tried to set down one solution to our current predicament — one recommendation about what we might do differently if our democracy is to survive Trump and everything he represents.

We could, of course, try to restore our country by rebuilding the same old structures that Trump has put to the torch. President Biden attempted just that — a return to normalcy, a belief in institutions and what they can do, warts and all. That proved not quite enough to avert a second Trump presidency, but who is to say that the Biden approach might not prove sufficient next time, certainly if enough people are disillusioned again with four more years of Trump? That, however, is a big risk and not a long-term solution.

There is an alternative: to use new tools to make our democratic structures more resilient to the next incendiary demagogue. Fortunately for us, other countries have sought to solve the same types of issues we are confronting, and have succeeded in various ways. In particular, Brazil, France, and Germany provide useful models of countries that have taken great strides toward shoring up their systems against demagogues who would seek to use lies to destroy democracy. These countries saw that trying to return to some halcyon, prelapsarian era would be a fool's errand, so instead they fortified their legal systems to avert any new conflagration. Can we, like these and other nations, confront foundational damage and devise reforms? Can we adapt their solutions to an American context, putting a stop to political lies and liars before it's too late?

One thing is certain: as I write these words, the crisis is upon us. We have no choice but to face it.

CHAPTER I

THE HONESTY CRISIS

We are a nation awash in lies.

Nowhere is this truer than in the political arena. For sure, more than one of our nation's leaders has been guilty of spinning the truth, but no one is guiltier in this regard than Donald Trump. He has made claims as absurd and xenophobic as immigrants eating pets or as racist as the origins of Barack Obama's birth with abandon and impunity. During Trump's first term, the *Washington Post* kept a running tally of over 30,000 presidential utterances that they catalogued as false or misleading — a prodigious average of 20.9 each day. The *Washington Post* scorecard was discontinued in Trump's second term, not because of any reformation in reported truthfulness by our chief executive, but I suspect because of the widely reported capitulation of that venerated institution by its owner.

Remarkably, millions of Americans swallow whole and endlessly regurgitate Trump's utterances. Take his boldest and most pernicious political lie: the claim that the 2020 presidential election was stolen from him. In one poll, roughly a third of Americans said that they believe the election outcome was the result of fraud, and approximately 69 percent of Republicans hold that belief.

This in spite of the fact that Trump promised the electorate that he would reveal a "Large, Complex, Detailed but Irrefutable REPORT" of election fraud, but then did not do so. Trump called off the press conference where he was to adduce this proof, claiming that his lawyers advised him not to do so. That strains credulity. Trump is hardly known for following legal counsel: he was alleged in the Mar-a-Lago documents case to have completely disregarded the common-sense advice that he return government documents to the government. And to date, although he's out of legal peril because that case was dismissed due to his reelection, he still has not revealed the "Irrefutable" evidence of election fraud. As there would be no political reason not to make such evidence public, and every reason to do so, I can only conclude that the proof never existed.

Just as the obvious untruth of statements such as this don't seem to matter to the majority of President Trump's supporters, neither do they matter to the American legal system: there is no criminal law that makes Trump's election fraud lie illegal. No civil law imposes any sanction on such falsehoods, either, such as disqualifying politicians who propagate them from running for elected office. Free and fair elections are the bedrock of our democratic system, and so is a shared belief that we have such elections. Yet Trump can — and does — lie to the public about them flagrantly, while remaining immune from legal accountability.

This is anomalous: our legal system penalizes all sorts of other lies and liars. Indeed, it metes out stiff punishments for many other, lesser lies told by many other, lesser mortals. I know from personal experience: during over two decades as a government lawyer, I prosecuted many a defendant for their criminal lies.

One of the most memorable of those cases involved Kenneth Lay, the chairman and chief executive officer of Enron, a Fortune no. 7 public company. In 2000, its final full year in business, Enron reported revenue of over $100 billion — that is, with a "b." In the fall of 2001 it imploded in an accounting scandal, and by December of that same year, it filed for bankruptcy. Its precipitous demise uncovered what was then the largest corporate fraud in American history. The company went down in history as the "crooked E" — a play on the Enron logo, which depicted a large multicolor "E" tilted to one side.

I was a leader of the Enron Task Force, which was created by the Department of Justice to investigate the company's collapse. This was in the halcyon days when the Republican administration of President George W. Bush left the DOJ free to determine without fear or favor the appropriate investigative and prosecutorial course to take, regardless of political consequences.

After sifting through the rubble of what had been the Enron Corporation, and "flipping" cooperating Enron witnesses as we progressed up the corporate ladder to the C suite, we were able to obtain a grand jury indictment charging Lay with fraud.

Our theory of the case was disarmingly simple. We compared Lay's rosy public statements about the state of Enron with what he knew at the time about the actual internal data. There were numerous private red flags that Enron was circling the drain, but the company's public statements gave no hint of that. One vignette captured this duality: at an internal Enron meeting in which Lay was being brought up to speed on a whiteboard on the latest looming internal crisis, Lay was reported to have stopped the briefing, saying that he didn't want to see it because he was about to attend a public financial analyst call.

Under US law, it is a crime for Lay, an employee of a publicly traded organization like Enron, to knowingly and intentionally tell a material lie about the company. Lay's deception resulted in multiple criminal charges and two trials based on his deceptive conduct. In both trials, the task force presented evidence of the divorce between private fact and public fiction. Lay was found guilty but died not long after the verdicts, and before he was to be sentenced. The law required the criminal cases be dismissed, as Lay did not have the opportunity to exhaust his right to appeal the verdicts for error. (Although there was rampant speculation that Lay killed himself rather than face jail, the evidence is to the contrary. Lay actually died of a massive heart attack.)

Kenneth Lay was not the only Enron executive to face prosecution for deception. Jeffrey Skilling — the CEO before Lay — was similarly held to account civilly and criminally for his intentional distortions, not only while he was CEO but also after he abruptly stepped down. Skilling had been Enron's CEO for less than a year when he suddenly resigned in August 2001. He explained at the time that his leaving had nothing to do with any concern about turmoil within Enron; it was to spend more time with his family — a tired refrain even back in 2001. When the company spectacularly imploded just a couple months later, the Securities and Exchange Commission sought to examine this dubious story. Skilling was subpoenaed to testify. He was asked why, if he was unaware of imminent and intractable problems at Enron, he had sold so many of his Enron shares in mid-September 2001, just weeks before it imploded. Skilling explained that the sales had nothing to do with the state of Enron, and everything to do with the state of the American stock market after the horrific attacks on the United States on September 11, 2001. Skilling testified that he sold out of concern that the market would drop dramatically as a result.

That story was plausible but for one inconvenient fact. Skilling placed an order to sell hundreds of thousands of shares of Enron stock just before, not after, the 9/11 attack. The SEC had the recording of his sell order to prove it. That led one of the dogged FBI agents with whom I worked on the Enron investigation to quip that Skilling was either guilty of perjury or was one of the 9/11 terrorists. Skilling was convicted of securities fraud and other charges by the same jury that convicted Lay.

Enron shareholders used the exact same fraud theory to sue Lay, Skilling, and other Enron executives and board members civilly under the securities laws. Given the criminal convictions, this was a fairly easy lift: civil law requires a lesser showing than criminal law, which requires proof beyond a reasonable doubt to be found unanimously, given that the government can take away a person's liberty. Civil law requires only a showing that something is more likely than not, what we lawyers term a "preponderance of the evidence." Although, to be fair, civil securities laws have additional requirements that the criminal law does not have. In any event, Enron's shareholders recovered tens of millions, but still only recouped pennies on the dollar compared to the financial harm that the crime had caused, not to mention the damage generally to the economy and the anguish resulting from losing precious savings.

This disconnect between knowing one thing and proclaiming another is a leitmotif in fraud cases, whether civil or criminal. I used to head up the Fraud Section at the Department of Justice, and we relied on this repeatedly in our financial investigations. When we successfully prosecuted the German car company Volkswagen, it was based on the company's publicly professing to produce "green" cars that passed various environmental standards, whereas in fact it was widely known within the company, including at the very top of its leadership, that it had simply cheated on the regulatory tests. It defrauded the public and polluted the earth simultaneously. We see a similar phenomenon at play in the world of sports — the athlete who juices his public performance by secretly taking prohibited drugs, just like Volkswagen and Enron enhanced their market performance with the false perception of internal health.

I had encountered this dichotomy between what defendants know to be true and what they state publicly while prosecuting mob bosses at the start of my career in the United States Attorney's Office in Brooklyn. For decades, Vincent Gigante, the head of the Genovese Family — the most powerful of the five New York Italian organized crime families—pretended to be incompetent. He paraded around Greenwich Village in a shoddy, threadbare, cotton bathrobe and days of stubble. As a result, a New York City tabloid nicknamed Gigante the "Oddfather." When Rudy Giuliani's federal prosecution office in Manhattan brought the "Commission case" against all the leaders of the five families in the 1980s, Gigante was conspicuously absent from the charges. He had checked himself into a hospital just days earlier, having been given an inside tip that the indictment was coming down.

I was assigned to the Gigante criminal investigation in the late 1990s. Gigante had by then ruled over the Genovese family for years, with impunity. Our first task was to prove that he was competent to stand trial. Otherwise, the criminal charges against Gigante would continue to languish while he remained at large, running the Genovese Family.

To prove his competence, we were able to get rare insight into Gigante's behavior in private. Gigante had a wife and family in New Jersey, but also a girlfriend in New York. In an odd quirk, both his wife and girlfriend were named Olympia. Gigante had bought his girlfriend Olympia a swanky Upper East Side town house. Each night for several months, FBI Special Agent Charles Beaudoin went to the roof of a neighboring school from which he could see into the back of the town house. He took contemporaneous notes memorializing his observations of

Gigante reading the paper, counting money, and speaking with visitors — all at a time when his doctors said he was virtually catatonic and incapable of such activities.

The vignette that I thought best encapsulated the gap between Gigante's public "crazy act" and his private sanity was revealed when I asked Charlie on the witness stand at the competency hearing if he ever saw Gigante in a bathrobe inside the town house. "Yes," he said. I asked him if he also had seen Gigante in a bathrobe on the streets of New York. Charlie said that he had. "Can you compare that bathrobe with the one in the town house?" I asked. Charlie then described the inside bathrobe as a plush, white, Brooks Brothers–type robe. I thought the visual contrast between this perfectly normal inside bathrobe and the disheveled, threadbare one for public consumption would present indelible images to help to seal his fate.

Undaunted by this testimony at the competency hearing, Gigante's famed defense counsel, Barry Slotnick, first tried to show that Charlie's eyesight was so poor that he could not have seen what he claimed. Slotnick went to the back wall of the long, dark, wood and green marble courtroom. The witness box in which the FBI agent was sitting was at the other end, a good twenty yards or so away, which Charlie said was about the distance he had been from the back of Olympia's town house. Slotnick held up what appeared to be US currency and asked Charlie to identify it. Without missing a beat, Charlie said it was a $10 bill.

"Correct," intoned the district judge, who took the bill from Slotnick and marked it as an exhibit. Undaunted, Slotnick held up some more currency. Again, Charlie identified it; this time it was a $20. The judge again marked it as an exhibit, but could not refrain from asking Slotnick, rhetorically, "How much money are you planning on losing?"

Slotnick changed tactics. Isn't it possible, he argued to the judge, that Gigante is feigning being competent, when he in fact is incompetent? "Haven't you heard of that ever happening?" he asked. Before anyone could respond to Slotnick's new position, Jimmy Breslin — the famed grizzled *Daily News* reporter who had been covering the proceedings from the spectator gallery — exclaimed in a failed stage whisper, "That describes the whole world." And with that *bon mot*, the Gigante gig was up. Slotnick had not been able to shake the clear import of Charlie's testimony exposing publicly for the first time the private truth of Gigante's crazy act.

At the conclusion of the hearing, thanks to Charlie's testimony and that of former senior La Cosa Nostra mobsters like Sammy Gravano about their private dealings with Gigante, the court declared Gigante competent to stand trial. He was later convicted on all counts by a jury. Gigante would even later admit, when he pleaded guilty to obstructing justice, that he had feigned mental illness to avoid prosecution. In other words, he had engaged in a public crazy act, when he privately was running a crime syndicate.

This private vs. public split can be readily applied to Trump's claim of election fraud in the 2020 presidential election. "We won this election and we won it by a landslide." Trump made this and similar public statements starting as early as November 2016 and continuing to the present. He continued in this vein from that day until this:

"I won the popular vote if you deduct the millions of people who voted illegally."

(November 27, 2016)

"There is NO WAY Biden got 80,000,000 votes!!!"

(November 26, 2020)

"This is the greatest fraud in the history of our country."

(November 29, 2020)

"Tremendous evidence pouring in on voter fraud. There has never been anything like this in our Country!"

(December 15, 2020)

"VOTER FRAUD IS NOT A CONSPIRACY THEORY, IT IS A FACT!!!"

(December 24, 2020)

"The 2020 election was a total FRAUD! The evidence is MASSIVE and OVERWHELMING."

(June 20, 2025)

"Watch how totally dishonest the California Prop Vote is! Millions of Ballots being 'shipped.'"

(October 26, 2025)

"The Unconstitutional Redistricting Vote in California is a GIANT SCAM in that the entire process, in particular the Voting itself, is RIGGED."

(November 4, 2025)

Although Trump repeatedly claims in public that he lost the 2020 election only because of fraud, Jack Smith and the January 6th Committee laid out in detailed reports that he privately had been made aware that he lost the election — and knew he had. An aide testified that he even admitted the loss privately. Indeed, two of Trump's biggest supporters provided evidence that his public election lie was planned in advance of the election results, as a failsafe that he could use if he lost.

The proof that Trump knowingly lied about the election is compelling. Specifically, Special Counsel Jack Smith detailed such evidence in two lengthy documents: a 45-page indictment, and a 137-page final report with 1,889 pages of supporting testimony and exhibits. The House of Representatives Select Committee on January 6th similarly compiled an 814-page report laying out its findings. Smith and the January 6th Committee conclude that Trump was aware of the following:

> Trump's senior lawyers at the Department of Justice and the White House, including Attorney General Bill Barr and his top two attorneys, Jeffrey Rosen and Richard Donoghue, as well as his White House counsel, Pat Cipollone, all told him that there was no evidence of election fraud that would have changed the outcome. Barr memorably testified that he told Trump the claim was "bullshit."

> Trump's own campaign staff, including people tasked with looking for evidence of material fraud, told him that there was no such evidence to support his claims.

> Chris Krebs, the head of Trump's Cybersecurity and Infrastructure Security Agency, stated publicly that the election was "the most secure in American history." Trump then fired Krebs (and has since retaliated against him by pulling his security clearance and by denigrating him in his own bespoke executive order).

State officials called by Trump disputed that there was election fraud. One famous incident involved taping the president importuning the secretary of state of Georgia to find the precise number of votes for him to prevail. (It speaks volumes that these officials understood that a tape would be needed to prove what was said.)

A staff member reported that Trump privately acknowledged that he had lost the election — saying that he would leave a thorny issue to the next guy and commenting about Biden, "Can you believe I lost to this f'in guy?"

Trump's own vice president, Mike Pence, did not believe that their ticket won.

Pence always struck me as a perfect trial witness to show the jury how a politician with a modicum of decency and a sense of truth behaves after losing an election. He provides the "control" for the Trump science experiment. Two people were on the same Republican ticket, each with the same interest to win, and each with similar sources of information. Both lost. But only one publicly denied it.

If this case had ever gone to trial, defense counsel for Donald Trump may have argued that his client was simply overoptimistic or self-deluded — that he was wrong, but not lying, in other words. That defense would be in considerable tension with Trump's claim that he had dispositive proof of fraud, but none has been forthcoming (even in court cases challenging the election, where one would think it might be advanced if it existed). And in tension with the reports that Trump contemplated making the fraud claim even before the alleged fraud occurred. And consider the following vignette: On January 5, 2021, Trump and Pence talked privately, and Pence said he could not go along with Trump's plan. Trump told Pence that he would have to criticize him for refusing to put off counting the electoral votes the next day. Just hours later, Trump issued the following statement: "The Vice President and I are in total agreement that the Vice President has the power to act." This is precisely the opposite of what Pence says occurred.

The election lie had a deadly impact the very next day. On January 6, Trump repeated the election lie in a lengthy speech before a crowd of his supporters at the Ellipse, a park just south of the White House. "They want to steal the election." "This election was stolen from you, from me, and from the country." "We will never give up, we will never concede." Remembering to say that the protestors should "peacefully and patriotically" make their voices heard, Trump then said what could have been readily understood to be the opposite: "We fight like hell. And if you don't fight like hell, you're not going to have a country anymore."

No wonder the mob wanted to "hang Mike Pence" after Trump misleadingly built up their expectations. The Department of Justice during the Biden administration would cite these public claims and exhortations as the catalyst for the January 6 insurrection. Numerous people who were later charged in connection with the events on January 6 would say that they believed what Trump was saying — it had led them to "fight like hell," to attack the Capitol building, to defecate in its hallways, to destroy and defile the seat of our government, and to physically assault police charged with protecting the building and us.

I always thought Trump was too clever by half when he dropped in the *peacefully* adjective at the Ellipse speech. To me, it was a tell that he knew exactly where the line was between the permissible espousing of ideas and the unlawful calling for obstructing Congress's vote-counting and even inciting violence. It is hard for me to interpret the single use of the word *peacefully* as doing any work other than trying to give himself plausible deniability. But it seems to me more accurately described as "implausible deniability," given the confluence of Trump being made aware of the fact that he lost the election, the lack of evidence of such fraud, Trump's later inaction even in the face of a mortal threat to his vice president, and his later complete embrace of the J6 rioters who would eventually receive presidential pardons.

Unlike in the cases of Lay, Skilling, and Gigante, however, all of whom were charged, tried, and ultimately found guilty for their lies, the government was never able to test its allegations against Trump at trial. I attribute this to a toxic combination of actions and inaction by Attorney General Merrick Garland, the Supreme Court, and the Trump defense team, all of whom contributed to delays in the case — a slowdown that prevented it from being tried before the 2024 presidential election, after which Special Counsel Jack Smith filed a motion to dismiss the case, in line with a longstanding DOJ policy against prosecuting a sitting president.

But even without Trump's January 6 case proceeding to trial, we definitively know how American law deals with election lies — or rather, how it doesn't.

It is a crime to lie to shareholders. It is a crime to lie to Congress. But it is not a crime to lie to the public. Lies of that sort are not even subject to civil liability or regulation. Trump had been charged with obstructing the election, which is a crime — but there is no law against lying about an election, as Trump did on January 6 and has continued to do ever since.

Let that sink in: saying over and over again that an election was stolen — even if it's done with full knowledge that it wasn't — is not a crime. The Trump insurrection indictment makes this very point: not only does the filing not charge Trump with an election lie, it also explicitly says that under the law such a lie is not illegal. Instead, the election lie was only relevant as proof that could help to establish that Trump committed some *other* crime, such as obstructing Congress from counting electoral votes or violating civil rights by engaging in election interference. Those crimes — the ones with which Trump could be charged — are far more complicated to prove than a simple false statement charge; obstructing Congress has various complicated prerequisites for conviction — so-called elements that must each be proved beyond a reasonable doubt, and which the Supreme Court in *Fischer v. United States* concluded had to involve attempting to impair the availability or integrity of evidence in the election proceeding.

But the crime of making a false statement is straightforward and intuitive: Did the defendant intentionally lie about something material (i.e., something more than, say, their favorite color)? If so, that is enough to support a criminal charge in innumerable other contexts: lying to Congress, lying to a jury, lying in a civil deposition, lying to a federal agent in an interview (even when not under oath), lying on a bank form, and so forth.

All of these lies are criminalized under United States law; Congress has made them illegal.

Not so lying to the public.

It says a lot about America's value system that our choice of stock is legally protected from Kenneth Lay's lies, whereas no such protection exists for our ballot choice when it's the subject of false claims of fraud. What's more, the fact that Trump has faced no legal accountability for his false claims about the 2020 election has permitted him to repeat them to this day, and to do so from the highest office in the land — an "alternative facts" blitzkrieg that has had devastating consequences for our democracy.

DEMOCRACY AT STAKE

It is entirely predictable that if you permit people to get away with election lies, the lies metastasize. We can actually all see these consequences: recall that one-third of Americans have said that they believe the 2020 election was stolen — and two-thirds of Republicans say the same. Trump achieved this result without ever presenting evidence to support the contention. In fact, every court that has confronted the claim has rejected it. Trump was elected president nonetheless.

Of course, Trump was not the first to resort to lies — think about Bill Clinton's "I did not have sexual relations with Ms. Lewinsky," or Nixon's "I am not a crook." But those presidents paid varying prices for their lies, whereas our current president lies outlandishly, with legal impunity. And his success emboldens others to emulate the tactic.

Our body politic is now riddled with lies, misrepresentations, distortions, and half-truths that undermine our rights and democratic institutions. Most directly, the election fraud lie provides the origin story for whitewashing the entire January 6 attack. More than 1,500 J6 criminals have been set loose and heralded as patriots and "political prisoners." When defecating in the Capitol is glorified by our own leaders as patriotic, how can a representative democracy survive? The sad point is that defecation on a revered monument is the perfect symbol of Trumpism. And the election lie, with its insistence on denial of the establishment's reality and its upending of facts and process, is the oxygen that fans those destructive flames.

On the very first day of his second term, Trump used the election fraud lie to justify meticulously eradicating all J6 prosecutions, root and branch. Trump issued pardons for all the convicted January 6 defendants, describing their prosecution as a "grave national injustice." Trump pardoned all of them, regardless of whether they pleaded guilty or were found guilty by a jury, regardless of whether they assaulted police officers, and regardless of whether they were leaders of violent gangs like the Proud Boys and Oath Keepers. For those still awaiting trial, Trump ordered his Department of Justice to seek "dismissal with prejudice" of all charges (meaning the charges cannot ever be reinstated by a later administration).

JD Vance and Pam Bondi, Trump's attorney general nominee (after his nomination of Matt Gaetz crashed and burned), had tried to calm the waters before Trump's second inauguration by reassuring the press, wrongly as it happened, that the Trump administration could differentiate between the violent and nonviolent J6 offenders. Trump was not to be deterred with such niceties: all of the defendants received some form of legal absolution. Ed Martin, Trump's newly minted Pardon Attorney, later said the quiet part out loud, describing Trump's use of his constitutional pardon power as "no MAGA left behind."

A psychologist might suggest that Trump engaged in such behavior so as to bludgeon the perception of legitimacy of the criminal justice system. Trump, after all, is the first US president to be an adjudicated felon, having been tried and convicted of thirty-four felony counts in his former hometown of New York City. The blanket pardons had the effect of upending the legitimacy of our legal system — the key structure we have for resolving disputes.

The pardons serve another, even more direct purpose for Donald Trump. If Trump was a catalyst for the J6 events, the rebranding of that day as something to applaud, not to be ashamed of, helps Trump personally. Recasting the J6 defendants as MAGA *causes célèbres* is nothing more than a way to exculpate Trump for his central role in the whole affair.

Given a president's conclusive and exclusive pardon power under the US Constitution, the courts had no choice but to accept the pardons, and virtually no discretion to reject the dismissal of the pending criminal cases. Federal District Judge Tanya Chutkan captured the mood of the courthouse in Washington, DC, where judges of all political backgrounds had labored mightily to assure due process for all the J6 defendants. From the scores of trials in their courtrooms, the judges were keenly aware of the evidence establishing what had occurred that day. Judge Chutkan poignantly wrote:

> No pardon can change the tragic truth of what happened on January 6, 2021 … It cannot whitewash the blood, feces, and terror that the mob left in its wake. And it cannot repair the jagged breach in America's sacred tradition of peacefully transitioning power.

Unchastened, the Trump administration's Department of Justice went a step further. It moved to dismiss certain charges against J6 defendants even if the crimes were unrelated to the events on January 6, so long as the evidence of the crimes was discovered in the course of the January 6 investigation. One federal judge who had been appointed by Trump in his first term found that position remarkable. She noted that DOJ's reasoning would absolve someone of murder if the evidence happened to be found in the course of a January 6 investigation. She rejected the government's position, acknowledging that if Trump wanted to issue a pardon for that unrelated conduct he could, but that she would not allow it to be based on the J6 pardons. Trump then did just that, and expanded the conduct covered by a new pardon.

There was more to come: the vilification of the people who held the J6 defendants to account. The career law enforcement officers on the United States side of the "*v.*" in the caption "*United States v. Defendant*" were ousted. Not waiting for the confirmation of Pam Bondi and Todd Blanche as attorney general and deputy attorney general, respectively, the then–Acting Deputy Attorney General Emil Bove summarily caused the firing or transferring of numerous career prosecutors and FBI agents who had worked on the J6 cases. He demanded a list of all FBI personnel who worked on the cases — a list that would contain the names of thousands of people — in order to evaluate them for adverse personnel action. To add to the mendacity and shamelessness of this undertaking, Bove himself had supported investigation of the J6 attack when he had been a career prosecutor in the Manhattan US Attorney's office.

Bove's actions now appeared to recast the career public officials as part of a conspiracy to railroad innocent J6 defendants. The Trump administration used this falsehood to summarily purge prosecutors from the Department of Justice. Career public servants who worked for Special Counsel Jack Smith were fired without cause. To make matters worse, whereas normally experienced and decorated prosecutors like these men and women would land on their feet in the private sector, large law firms, euphemistically known as Big Law, won't touch various Smith team members as of this writing for fear of putting a target on their backs.

vilified numerous career FBI special agents with years of training and expertise. The career domestic terrorism FBI agent who headed the Salt Lake City, Utah, FBI field office was pushed out just weeks before the Charlie Kirk assassination. Needless to say, this was a time when such depth of knowledge was most needed. Walter Giardina (who worked for Special Counsels Smith and Mueller) was fired by FBI Director Kash Patel in spite of reported pleas from senior FBI leadership that Patel hold off because Giardina's wife — a ballet dancer who taught children with disabilities the joy of dance — was dying of cancer. In fact, she died shortly before Giardina's firing.

What kind of person would decide to fire a grieving husband under these circumstances? And Trump piled on with invective, labeling Giardina a "DIRTY COP!" — but again with no actual evidence to back up the epithet. Not long after, the FBI leaders who reported that they had tried to have Patel show a modicum of humanity toward Giardina were themselves fired. Again, I would ask: What type of person creates an environment that makes such actions acceptable, and not the subject of universal scorn and discipline? These are the people running our country now. And these are but a few examples.

The firing and denigration of the public servants who worked on the J6 cases ignores two facts: there is no evidence the election was stolen, and even assuming that the J6 rioters believed the lie that it was stolen, that did not justify taking the law into their own hands and committing crimes, high and low, violent and nonviolent. They could go to court (which some did and lost, repeatedly) or they could protest peacefully (which some also did). Engaging in violence and physically attacking law enforcement were not legal options, even if you believed the election lie.

The administration's lies have mushroomed, the rot spreading to many other domains. In the immigration context, lies are fueling the mistreatment of tens of thousands of people. Trump has stoked xenophobia at least since first announcing his presidential aspirations, whether it be the birther lie about President Obama or his denigrating a judge — an American citizen — as a "Mexican" who consequently could not obey his judicial oath of office to fairly adjudicate a civil case to which Trump was a party.

Trump claimed that we were being invaded by murderers and rapists from other countries. The facts were beside the point: numerous studies have found that immigrants commit crimes at lower rates than native-born Americans. A study out of Texas concurred, finding immigrants were arrested at half the rate of US-born citizens for drug and violent crimes, and a quarter of the rate for property crimes.

In his second term in office, Trump continued smearing immigrants and stoking xenophobia in an executive order that announced without citing any factual support that the United States was being invaded by a Venezuelan gang called Tren de Aragua. Usually an invasion is something we would have seen and experienced ourselves, so the news of a Venezuelan invasion was surely a surprise to us all. One federal judge thought it fanciful for the administration to try to claim that a law involving an actual British invasion of this country in 1812 could justify an imagined current TdA military invasion. You know you have come up with a whopper when even the ultraconservative federal Fifth Circuit Court of Appeals rejects your claim that there is an "invasion" justifying summarily extracting people from the country without a hearing.

In a sign of how far we are from a government operating based on facts, another court, when confronted with the question of whether one husband and wife were members of the TdA gang, found that the government had not even established that basic fact, which is of course a necessary prerequisite to justify removing them as being a part of TdA (even if TdA were actually engaged in an invasion). As to the wife, the court noted that the government had established no facts that justified concluding she was in TdA; with respect to the husband, the proof consisted solely of being married to his wife.

Lies about immigrants have even been used to target immigrant children. Over Labor Day weekend 2025, the administration tried to summarily extract hundreds of minors from the United States without any judicial process whatsoever. Late that Saturday night, ICE agents went to shelters and foster care homes to round up hundreds of children, forcing them out of their beds in the middle of the night. The Trump administration then hastily put scores of these children on planes bound for Guatemala. Recall that when the administration did this with adults and dumped them in shackles in a God-forsaken prison in El Salvador, the Supreme Court held 9–0 that it violated their due process rights. These children, too, were entitled to due process before removal, and were covered by a congressional law specifically governing a judicial process that had to be followed to remove children from the country. This did not protect them from an administration that did not follow the law.

The administration, it turns out, did not adhere to the facts, either. Thanks only to the fast work of lawyers for some of the children was a court alerted on early Sunday morning as to what ICE was doing. The federal judge who was on emergency duty that weekend held an immediate hearing. Unbowed, the Trump administration resorted to false claims to the court to justify its conduct. The government, far from being contrite, followed the old adage that the best defense is a good offense. The children's lawyers should be scolded, the government lawyer intoned, for the "fairly outrageous" effort to interfere with the "reunification" of the children with their parents, which the Trump DOJ lawyer claimed he had been told one or both parents had requested.

The federal judge noted that the lawyers for the plaintiffs disputed that government assertion. For instance, one child had submitted an affidavit that said her mother was dead (and thus could not have sought reunification) and that her father had abused her as a child. There was, the judge noted, an important factual disagreement: Was the Trump administration merely seeking to reunify children at the request of one or both parents, as it claimed without any supporting proof? Or were the plaintiffs, who had submitted sworn evidence to support their position, correct that no such reunification had been requested? The issue was critical because the government said that it was not bound by the congressional statute on removals because what it was doing was "repatriations and reunifications" of children with their parents at their own request.

The court pressed pause, stopping the government from removing the children, at least temporarily, until the facts and legal issues could be resolved at a hearing. Rather than await these determinations, the White House pounced on the judge. "The Biden judge is effectively kidnapping these migrant children and refusing to let them return home to their parents in their home country," Trump aide Stephen Miller wrote on X that day.

The court hearing came just days later. The assigned judge, District of Columbia federal judge Timothy Kelly, was not a "Biden judge"; he was appointed by Trump in his first term. But that did not affect his adherence to his oath of office to administer justice without fear or favor. Judge Kelly rejected the government's claim, made just days earlier, that it was seeking reunification with the consent of the parents. In light of a report from the attorney general of Guatemala, the government now had to do a complete 180 and announced that it did not in fact have the consent of the parents. The change was not lost on Judge Kelly, who wrote about the government's claim of reunification thus:

But that explanation [of alleged reunification] crumbled like a house of cards about a week later. There is no evidence before the Court that the parents of these children sought their return. To the contrary, the Guatemalan Attorney General reports that officials could not even track down parents for most of the children whom Defendants [the Trump administration personnel and agencies] found eligible for their "reunification" plan. And none of those that were located had asked for their children to come back to Guatemala.

The Guatemalan report belied the factual claim by the Trump administration that it was simply reuniting hundreds of children with their parents and doing so at the parents' request. Notably, the government did not provide the Guatemalan attorney general's report to the court, although it is hard for me to believe that the government did not know about it. Indeed, if it did not, that is just as damning, since our government claimed to have been working in coordination with Guatemala, and its entire legal justification rested on facts that it had not, but could have, verified. The report came to light only because the press alerted the public to it. And when the report came to light, the Trump administration lawyers neither disputed it nor suggested to Judge Kelly anything to explain why it had represented the opposite just days earlier.

All of this deception was undertaken to remove children without due process, when a perfectly good legal system was available to the government. But rather than beginning removal proceedings under the law, the government ignored both the law and the facts. And in doing so, it revealed a darker issue.

The mistreatment of these Guatemalan children, of the adult TdA "suspects," and of many others have a common taproot: lies that depict the undocumented and immigrants as something less than human. That these people are invariably from Black and Brown communities undergirds so much of the White nationalist message from this administration. "They" poison the American body politic and are to be removed, like some dreaded cancerous tumor. The political bet is that there won't be enough people who care about due process when the people whose due process rights have been violated are not White, or who may be convincingly depicted as unsympathetic. This gambit explains the administration's extraordinary public effort to vilify the people being summarily extracted.

The notorious case of Kilmar Armando Abrego Garcia is sadly just one illustration of this phenomenon. On March 12, 2025, the Trump administration illegally seized Abrego Garcia as he was leaving his job in Baltimore and then sent him to El Salvador. This violated a prior court order that specifically prohibited his being sent to El Salvador, because he had established to a US judge a legitimate basis to fear retribution if he were sent there. To make matters worse, after being extracted from the United States without a hearing, Abrego Garcia was not free when he got to El Salvador: he was sent to rot in the CECOT prison with no known prospect for release. Once Abrego Garcia was stashed in a foreign prison, the government claimed it could not bring him back. This, in spite of the fact that the United States had paid hundreds of thousands of dollars to El Salvador to imprison him and others.

Not only is that position fanciful, it is cruel. It is inconceivable to me that any DOJ leader for whom I have worked over numerous Republican and Democratic administrations would ever react this way. Imagine going to your boss and reporting that you had just removed someone from the country illegally, against a court order. And that person was now in prison in the foreign country as a result of your illegal action. Any decent and moral person would ask how fast you could get him back to the United States. Did the Trump administration do that? No. It took a decidedly different tack: tarnish the immigrant so people would not care about what the government had done to him.

The DOJ lawyer on the Abrego Garcia case, Erez Reuveni, has provided direct evidence that he was instructed to call Abrego Garcia a terrorist, but he refused unless he was given evidence of that — which is to say, he was not willing to lie to the court. Reuveni was no Biden holdover; he was a career lawyer who had argued many a Trump administration immigration case and had been recently promoted by Trump's attorney general. Nevertheless, he was promptly fired by that same attorney general. She then went on the national airwaves to besmirch Abrego Garcia herself. The reason was purely political, not legal:

Why should you care about the niceties of constitutional rights (and whether DOJ violated a court order) when we are talking about removing a bad and dangerous person?

The sins go deep: as Attorney General, Bondi must know that whether Abrego Garcia is a terrorist or not is entirely irrelevant to the legal issue of whether DOJ violated the preexisting court order. Abrego Garcia was entitled to a hearing before being seized and removed from the country. The government would have to meet its burden of proof and Abrego Garcia would be able to challenge the facts and law. That in fact is why we have criminal trials. All defendants are entitled to due process and require the government to prove guilt beyond a reasonable doubt. The government doesn't get to skip that step just because the attorney general announces on *Fox News* that she thinks you are a bad person.

Thankfully, the Trump administration's new tactic was soundly rejected by the appellate court overseeing the case. The opinion was authored by a revered conservative jurist, Judge J. Harvie Wilkinson — someone whom the right views in much the same way that the left thinks about Ruth Bader Ginsburg. He noted the most obvious point first, which now needed to be said given what the Trump administration was doing: "The government asserts that Abrego Garcia is a terrorist and a member of MS-13. Perhaps, but perhaps not. Regardless, he is still entitled to due process. If the government is confident of its position, it should be assured that position will prevail in proceedings" to remove Abrego Garcia from the country.

As for the government's attempts to wash its hands of Abrego Garcia by claiming that it was powerless to bring him back, Judge Wilkinson was having none of it. "There is no question that the government screwed up here," he bluntly penned. In common-sense language, for all to read and understand, he said that "the government has conceded that Abrego Garcia was wrongly or 'mistakenly' deported. Why then should it not make what was wrong, right?" Judge Wilkinson was not alone. One of his judicial colleagues excoriated the government for punishing Reuveni for carrying out his duty to the court to be truthful. As lawyers, we are all trained that we have a duty to zealously advocate for our clients, but that is secondary to our "duty of candor" to judges as "officers of the court."

Judge Wilkinson did not hide his fury at the lawlessness and prevarication he was witnessing.

The government is asserting a right to stash away residents of this country in foreign prisons without the semblance of due process that is the foundation of our constitutional order. Further, it claims in essence that because it has rid itself of custody that there is nothing that can be done. This should be shocking not only to judges, but to the intuitive sense of liberty that Americans far removed from courthouses still hold dear.

What was at stake in Abrego Garcia's case, he concluded, was the very rule of law itself: "It takes no small amount of imagination to understand that this is a path of perfect lawlessness." Judge Wilkinson ended by urging the White House to turn back before it was too late. It was, he noted,

> all too possible to see in this case an incipient crisis, but it may present an opportunity as well. We yet cling to the hope that it is not naïve to believe our good brethren in the Executive Branch perceive the rule of law as vital to the American ethos. This case presents their unique chance to vindicate that value and to summon the best that is within us while there is still time.

But the conservative judge's heartfelt plea was met by crude, juvenile derision by the White House. With the words "Fixed it for you, @NYTimes," the White House tweeted a doctored version of a *New York Times* headline about the case. It crossed out the word "wrongly" and "Maryland Man," replacing the latter with a description of Abrego Garcia as an "MS-13 Illegal Alien," after which it scrawled the words "Who's Never Coming Back."

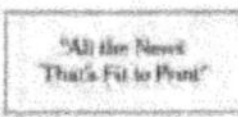

The New York Times

BREAKING NEWS

Senator Meets With ~~Wrongly~~ Deported Maryland Man in El Salvador

The bitter irony in all of this is that, of all our presidents, Donald Trump should best understand the value of due process. Just because the government asserts something does not mean that it is true; the government needs to present proof to substantiate its accusations. In all four of his criminal cases, Trump was accorded the due process that he is now denying countless others.

In addition to the erosion of due process rights in America, courts have determined that flat-out misrepresentations are now fueling the effort to send the military into our cities — at least our "blue" cities. The Trump administration claims that it is unable to contain the violence in these "war-ravaged" places with normal law enforcement efforts. It was time to call in the marines. And the national guard. Yet another federal judge summed up the factual claims by Trump and his administration as "untethered to the facts." That is a not-so-subtle way of saying that they were a bunch of lies. The judge, appointed by none other than Donald Trump in his first term, adhered to her oath of office to decide the case without fear or favor to any party. This did not prevent Steven Miller decrying her decision as being part of a "legal insurrection." Deputy Attorney General Todd Blanche told a Federalist Society gathering it was time for a "war" on these judges.

The creep of lies and deception into our government policies goes far beyond the claims of election fraud, the tarring of immigrants, and use of the military domestically. Lies abound: about COVID and vaccines, about Russian interference in the election, about having rid the world of ISIS. More recently, America's attacks on the sovereignty of Venezuela, whether by blowing up boats offshore or by abducting its president, have been fueled by the administration's pretextual claim that it is taking these actions to thwart drugs entering the United States — something at odds with, among other things, the US decisions to remain in Venezuela to run its oil industry and to pardon the Honduran president who was convicted of conspiring to import 400 tons of cocaine into the United States.

This kind of political deceit, and the actions it supports, have risked our national security by making us pariahs in the international community. For instance, the Trump administration's assaults on Venezuela are a sign of the disregard of international law, which most reputable experts believe has been violated. But these actions also hurt us in more direct ways. Promulgating lies about the efficacy of medical cures for diseases, for instance, does not make the disease go away — just the opposite. Policies based on falsehoods, such as using quack theories to justify denying funds to basic research into promising medical science, hurts the health of the entire nation. Denying the existence of a potent enemy, whether a disease, a nation state, or a terrorist group, is not an effective strategy to defeat that threat. It is fools' gold, serving to augment the false illusion of Donald Trump's success in the same manner that Kenneth Lay's lies did about Enron.

In addition to outright affirmative lies, deception has taken another important form. The Trump administration has caused a distraction when facts it would prefer to remain unscrutinised are disclosed to the public. In the Abrego Garcia case, counsel for the former government prosecutor filed a whistleblower complaint alleging that the DOJ attorney was fired for disclosing the truth to the court. The head of the Bureau of Labor Statistics was fired when she disclosed poor economic news. This was done even though we were never told what was wrong with her calculations. In fact, her calculations had been lauded as correct when she announced positive economic news. What had changed, other than the misalignment of this official's facts with the White House's preferred narrative? In cases such as this, the Trump administration is betting that, by killing the messenger, they can also kill the message. In Trump world, "hear no evil, see no evil" means that there *is* no evil.

We saw something similar when Trump derided the official reporting on the number of COVID cases in

America by protesting that the statistics were high "only because of our big number testing." By this reasoning, if officials stopped counting COVID cases or didn't make the numbers public, then the public's perception of the problem would disappear, like children who cover their eyes and think they've become invisible. Taking down government websites and databases, altering historical facts in museums, privately exhorting the State of Georgia to magically "find" 11,780 votes, and extorting Ukraine to say that it was investigating a political opponent without disclosing the extortion that coerced the announcement of the investigation, all are a part of the honesty crisis.

Unchecked lies and deceptions are gutting our democracy. Judge Wilkinson's *cri de coeur* is one memorable warning about the damage wrought by these falsehoods. Many other judges have been ringing that same alarm bell, too. One such warning in particular sticks in my mind: that issued by the federal judge who presided over the case of Paul Manafort.

In retrospect, Manafort's crimes were emblematic of the lawlessness and deceit that would come to pervade both Trump administrations. Manafort served for several months as Trump's 2016 presidential campaign manager. In 2017, I was assigned by Special Counsel Robert Mueller to head the team overseeing the Manafort investigation.

Within a handful of months, two separate grand juries had indicted Manafort for a slew of crimes: bank and tax fraud, money laundering, witness tampering, making false statements to the Department of Justice, and violation of the Foreign Agents Registration Act ("FARA," which requires registration with the Department of Justice by any person working for a foreign actor who seeks to influence US policy). Manafort was ultimately convicted by a Virginia jury of eight of the charges, and he pleaded guilty shortly thereafter to two more charges in Washington, DC, where he admitted under oath his liability for all the outstanding charges in both indictments.

At the heart of most of the charges was Manafort's lying. He lied to banks, to the tax authorities, and to federal prosecutors at the Department of Justice through his own defense counsel (to whom he also lied). All those lies, unlike lies by politicians to the public, are the subject of criminal statutes. Congress has decreed that all these lies are illegal, and that allowed us to hold Manafort accountable.

At Manafort's sentencing on March 13, 2019, District Judge Amy Berman Jackson noted that it was difficult "to overstate the number of lies and the amount of fraud and the extraordinary amount of money involved." Manafort, she noted, hid his income

> from the American people who pay their share
> of taxes so that the government, the military, the

national security apparatus, the veterans hospitals and all of the other functions that ordinary people rely on, can operate. Why? Not to support a family, but to sustain a lifestyle at the most opulent and extravagant level possible. More houses than a family can enjoy, more suits than one man can wear.

Judge Jackson concluded that Manafort's lies to federal investigators on the Mueller team had another important deleterious effect — thwarting the ability to investigate Russian interference in the 2016 election and any coordination with the Trump campaign. She rejected the speculation by Manafort at the time that there was no "collusion" with Russia, noting that it was "not particularly persuasive to argue that an investigation hasn't found anything when you lied to the investigators."

Before concluding her sentence, Judge Jackson had something else to say that has stayed with me. To survive, democracy requires the truth, and courts are where truth still matter. "Disregard for truth undermines our political discourse and it infects our policymaking. If the people don't have the facts, democracy can't work." With respect to how to sift through the public cacophony of lies, Jackson observed: "Court is one of those places where facts still matter."

Yet when it comes to political lies that deny, distort, or hide those facts and thus aim a dagger at the heart of democracy, the courts can't do this essential job. Because we have not let them.

Manafort was sentenced to a total of seven and a half years in jail, but Trump pardoned him in 2021 on his way out the door of the Oval Office. Manafort had served slightly less than two years in prison.

CHAPTER 3

THE MARKETPLACE OF IDEAS

How did we become a country where political lies seemingly have no legal repercussions? Where lies are taken for granted, creating a vicious circle of distrust and cynicism between political leaders and the citizens who empower them?

The legal answer, if not the political one, can be traced to an analogy made popular by the famous jurist and Supreme Court Justice Oliver Wendell Holmes Jr. In the early twentieth century, he penned a famous dissenting opinion in a case involving men convicted for distributing leaflets opposing United States intervention in the Russian Bolshevik revolution. Holmes famously wrote that the defendants' speech should not have been subject to prosecution. "The ultimate good desired," he wrote, "is better reached by free trade in ideas — that the best test of truth is the power of the thought to get itself accepted in the competition of the market." Holmes's dissent never actually used the phrase "marketplace of ideas," but later Supreme Court cases adopted both that phrase and Holmes's market metaphor in its drive to expand free speech rights.

Holmes's insight made sense when applied to the case before him — a case about Americans' rights to publicly voice their opinions about whether the United States should play a role in an unfolding foreign event. It was protected free speech, but the speech at issue did not involve factual truth or falsity. It was the expression of a viewpoint. By definition, such an opinion is not provably true or false one way or the other. It just is. Allowing opinions like these to vie for favor in the public square is appropriate and fitting — part of the robust vision of our First Amendment.

But as often happens in the law, Holmes's words came to be invoked in circumstances far beyond those in which they were birthed. Today, political lies about facts are thought to be immune from regulation based on the inapt application of this early-twentieth-century Holmes dissenting opinion. Holmes's invocation of the "competition of the market" has been applied to the very different situations in which contested speech involves not opinions but rather hard, verifiable facts.

We should be able to keep faith with Holmes's admirable strong protection of subjective opinions without inflicting on our democracy unchecked lies and liars. While Darwin's "natural selection" may be a perfectly valid biological theory, it has little application to how the law should treat truth and lies, and thus no legal system should conceive of the battle between truth and lies as a Darwinian survival of the fittest. A majority of the populace might disbelieve the law of gravity, but Isaac Newton's apple is still going to fall from a tree.

In fact, the law does brush aside the marketplace of ideas metaphor in a wide variety of contexts when intentional factual lies are at issue. Kenneth Lay, Jeffrey Skilling, and Vincent Gigante can all attest to that. So, too, can the unlikely bedfellows of Roger Stone and James Comey — both charged with intentionally lying to Congress, which understandably Congress has criminalized. Martha Stewart was convicted of lying to federal investigators and Paul Manafort of lying to a bank — both also made crimes by congressional statute. Why should these lies be subject to legal restraint, but lies by politicians to the public get a pass?

Trump himself appears to be keenly aware of this distinction between legal and illegal lies — between lies that are protected by Holmes's "marketplace" concept and those that aren't. This struck me during his first impeachment trial in December 2019, when the US House of Representatives charged Trump with extorting Ukraine by means of withholding congressionally appropriated military aid. Trump was accused of trying to get Ukraine to announce that it was criminally investigating Joe Biden, one of his key political rivals at the time, so that he could use such an announcement against Biden in the upcoming election — and surely without disclosing to the American people that Ukraine's investigation was the result of this backroom arm-twisting. When all this came to light, Trump took to the airwaves to deny to the electorate that he had tried to engage in a *quid pro quo* from Ukraine — its announcement of a Biden investigation in exchange for his administration's release of the congressional funding. He said the call with Ukraine president Volodymyr Zelenskyy was "perfect."

What Trump did not do in this situation is telling: he did not say any of this under oath in Congress during the impeachment proceedings, even though he said it all publicly. Trump never even submitted a sworn, or even unsworn, declaration to Congress. Why not? I think it is because such statements might be prosecuted under the federal statute making it a crime to lie to Congress and to obstruct Congress — coincidentally, the exact crimes Trump has successfully directed be brought against his former FBI

Director James Comey. So Trump avoided lying in a congressional proceeding. Instead, Trump just made his dubious claims to the entire American public — and thanks to Holmes's marketplace concept and its legacy, he was able to do so with impunity.

This inconsistency in how we handle lies in our legal ecosystem is all the more striking when you consider that we do impose legal constraints on political lies when the lie is directed at a particular person. That is what defamation law is all about. Just ask Ruby Freeman and Wandrea' ArShaye "Shaye" Moss, the mother and daughter who brought a civil defamation lawsuit against Rudy Giuliani for falsely accusing them of tampering with the 2020 presidential election votes in Georgia. Giuliani's statements had resulted in intense national public vilification of the mother and daughter, and even death threats to them both. Does our legal system say that Giuliani's statements and the women's denials are left to fend for themselves in the wilderness of an imagined marketplace of ideas? No: the question of his assertions' veracity was resolved in court. A judge and jury held him legally responsible, and the jury awarded the women almost $150 million.

Another, even more direct example of a political lie being subject to regulation — that is, being exempt from Holmes's marketplace of ideas — comes from the Dominion Voting Systems defamation case. When Trump lost the 2020 election, an array of people, including media outlets like Fox, disseminated a conspiracy theory that the loss was due to Dominion machines being used to delete votes for Trump or switch votes to Biden. If true, this could have thrown the election to Biden, since over half the states in the country and Puerto Rico used voting machines or vote tabulation software developed by Dominion to count votes in their elections. But it wasn't true — and the company didn't have to wait for an imaginary marketplace to set the record straight.

In 2021, Dominion filed a civil case against individuals such as Rudy Giuliani, Sidney Powell, and Mike Lindell (the MyPillow CEO), and organizations including One American News Network and — most famously — Fox. It alleged that it had been defamed by their fostering and amplifying a conspiracy theory about its supposed election interference. In April 2023, just before the scheduled trial, Fox settled with Dominion for the eye-popping sum of $787.5 million.

Because the Dominion case was resolved prior to trial, we do not have the benefit of a jury verdict or, to be fair, an appellate court's assessment of the legal rulings that the trial court had issued in the course of the pretrial proceedings. Nevertheless, the case demonstrates the law's ability to hold a core election fraud lie to account. The trial court ruled that there was no doubt that the claim was utterly false. The judge found: "The evidence developed in this civil proceeding demonstrates that [it] is CRYSTAL clear that none of the [s]tatements relating to Dominion about the 2020 election are true." The huge settlement figure, arrived at only after both sides engaged in extensive discovery (the exchange of documents and deposing witnesses and experts), supports the conclusion that Fox was completely aware of that fact.

All of us who believe in facts were victims of the same 2020 election fraud claim that was the basis of this private civil defamation lawsuit. Such claims, of course, serve to fuel distrust in the electoral process generally and to shore up support for Trump specifically. He could be portrayed as a victim of election fraud and not as a "loser." As the Dominion trial judge concluded, it was "'well-known and understood by everybody in the business' that former President Trump would 'claim that the only way that he could lose the election was by fraud, or that the only way that he would not prevail would be if it was stolen . . . He had laid that predicate down throughout the spring and the summer.'"

But although, per the district judge's conclusions, we were all subject to this attempted fraud, only Dominion had a legal remedy available to it. The rest of us have no standing to sue over an election lie, because in the eyes of the law we are mere voters; the only reason that the election fraud lie was remediable in this civil case is because the people spreading it happened to blame a particular target, Dominion. Its attorneys were able to drag the lie into court by arguing that it was defamatory. That is, they could argue that lie had a direct financial effect on Dominion: by casting doubt on the company's integrity, the liars had rendered it all but unemployable in future elections.

Only this direct identification of Dominion had opened the courthouse doors to the case. If the election fraud claim had remained in the passive voice — for instance, if the people spreading it had simply claimed, as President Trump regularly does, that "election fraud happened" — then Dominion would have been powerless to fight it, at least under current law. By extension, unless a politician or political candidate is foolish enough to defame a specific person in the process of spreading lies about an election, the "marketplace of ideas" metaphor continues to bar the courthouse doors.

The marketplace analogy has proven itself to be particularly dangerous when it comes to political lies. Whatever marketplace exists for political speech, it almost assuredly is not going to be effective in sorting fact from fiction in this domain. Even if one believes that a purported marketplace of ideas works some, or even most, of the time to dispel the force of a political lie, that may not be good enough to prevent the lie from working. Politics today is often a game of inches. A candidate does not have to fool all of the people all of the time, to borrow from the famous quip attributed to Abraham Lincoln. You just need to fool enough of the people by election time. If enough citizens believe a falsehood enough to affect their votes, then the lie wins. The cynical politician knows this, and can lie safe in the knowledge that there is no legal forum to timely and adequately counteract it.

We don't have to wonder if this happens: we know that it does. The marketplace of ideas is not dulling the bite of Trump's election fraud lie. As we've seen, the marketplace failed approximately two-thirds of the group of Republicans whose support Trump needed to secure his party's nomination ahead of the 2024 elections; it also failed around one-third of the group (the general electorate) whose support he needed to secure the presidency again. Trump has not had to answer in court for this claim, even if Dominion has. Trump has not had to explain, under oath and subject to cross-examination, his factual basis for his assertion. What the public is left with, instead, are his hollow assertions and bumper-sticker labels — claims devoid of any actual evidence.

Whatever the efficacy of a marketplace of ideas in the early twentieth century, it has long since ceased to function. This is due, in part, to the fact that there have been vast changes in our communications systems since Holmes penned his dissent in 1919. Thanks to the Internet and social media, we live in a time where individuals have never had a greater ability to speak to wide audiences, unfiltered, and to be able to access others' unfiltered speech. There is no remotely comparable historical analogue to what we are experiencing; we are the first people to deal with this phenomenon, and we have no defense against its excesses. The vast array of speech we experience has turned into a cacophony.

In spite of our unique ability to speak today — or, indeed, because of it — we ironically have a less well-functioning marketplace of ideas than we did in Holmes's time or in the intervening decades. The days of three US television networks and their virtual hegemony over the news are long gone. There is no Walter Cronkite to unmask the charlatan, to alert us when "skim milk masquerades as cream," as Gilbert and Sullivan so charmingly phrased it. Nightly news broadcasts — indeed, all traditional news outlets — are in free fall among young viewers. YouTube and TikTok are on the rise as major sources of news, as are influencers with various journalistic pedigrees (or none at all). A 2024 Pew Research Center study found that 37 percent of young adults regularly get their news from influencers on social media platforms. Four in ten aged 18–29 regularly get their news from TikTok, compared to just 10 percent for those aged 50–64, and just 3 percent for those over 65.

The profusion of data is a problem for all of us. In science, for instance, researchers are struggling to keep up with the massive amount of new research. Younger scientists are no longer the driving force of novel discoveries, as it is taking longer and longer to develop sufficient expertise to make a breakthrough. In the Intelligence Community, analysts now have more data to process than they can handle, resulting in a huge and growing backlog. As then–FBI Director Robert Mueller observed to me when I was the FBI general counsel, the problem for law enforcement is no longer that we won't have information in our intelligence holdings about the next terrorist; rather, it is how to sift through the vast data to find the right nugget before an attack occurs.

Similarly, with no barrier to entry into the social media marketplace, the volume of data we encounter there is overwhelming. To be able to digest any of it, we often must rely on others to filter and distill it. This creates bubbles of information, often created and curated by people we've never met and algorithms far removed from anything that most of us can understand. Too often, these spheres result in the exact opposite of a marketplace of ideas: they produce repetitious orthodoxies for the people trapped inside of them, with no dissenting voices who might be able to penetrate the bubble to offer contrary, let alone truthful, information.

To be sure, there are still smart and ethical investigative journalists, but their place in the news ecosystem is hardly growing. The mainstream media may ferret out the political falsehood from the ground truth, but they no longer have the same reach to galvanize what is often referred to as a "court of public opinion." Between media outlets captured to promulgate one-sided stories (the successful Dominion case against Fox being a prime illustration) on the one hand, and the rise of the Wild West of social media feeds on the other, the so-called court of public opinion is an anachronism.

Here is a useful thought experiment: If Watergate were to occur today, would President Nixon be forced to resign? Would there be sufficient media coverage of the facts of his misconduct, or would media bubbles insulate enough Americans from the truth to allow Nixon to evade justice? That is not really much of a hypothetical question; the answer is unfolding before our eyes today. When the right heralds criminals found guilty for participating in the January 6, 2021, attack on the Capitol as political prisoners who did nothing wrong, and those who investigated them are labeled and treated as traitors, fiction has become fact, and fact, fiction.

History offers a rough but instructive analogy to what we are going through today. At the turn of the twentieth century, before the Red Scare and before the rise of Hitler, America had virtually no restrictions on who could run for elected offices (if you were a White man, that is). There were so many candidates that the choices were difficult for the average citizen to keep track of. This gave party bosses enormous power because they would put together bundles of candidates. This was aptly dubbed the "asparagus" voting system. The bosses correctly banked on there not being enough citizens with the time or inclination to do their own research on each individual candidate. Slates of candidates selected by bosses, not the voters, did the work for these busy members of the electorate.

Progressives tackled this problem by supporting ballot reform measures to reduce the power of party bosses like New York's infamous Boss Tweed. The new laws gave the people more of a voice in party nominations and restricted the flood of eligible candidates to only those with a sufficient showing of popular support. For instance, a candidate could be required to submit a petition with a minimum number of qualified voters from the prospective candidate's district.

Ironically, these ballot access restrictions served to enhance, not diminish, the power of the people over the political machines of the day. With fewer options at the polls, voters had greater power to make informed decisions. This might seem uncontroversial now, when ballot access petitions are commonplace, but it was not obvious at the turn of the twentieth century, nor was it easy to accomplish. Still, the reformers persisted, and today we all are the beneficiaries of their efforts.

Importantly, these ballot restrictions have been approved time and again by the Supreme Court, which has endorsed the Progressives' vision that the restrictions rendered the right to vote more meaningful, not less. "It seems to us that limiting the choice of candidates to those who have complied with state election law requirements," the Court wrote in one 1992 opinion, "is the prototypical example of a regulation that, while it affects the right to vote, is eminently reasonable." The Court observed that "common sense, as well as constitutional law," compels the conclusion that government must play an active role in structuring elections if "they are to be fair and honest and if some sort of order, rather than chaos, is to accompany the democratic processes."

The analogy to the current problem is plain: we are inundated with information now, too, only the source is digital media rather than teeming fields of political candidates. As in the early twentieth century, this profusion of data has real-world political consequences. We must increasingly rely on others, be they media outlets or social media algorithms, to sift through political information on our behalf. With a proliferation of partisan media outlets and balkanized social media feeds that permit the consumer to see and hear only preselected information, the "news" can serve to close our minds, not open them to other views and perspectives as Holmes anticipated in his "marketplace," and Karl Popper envisioned in his "open society." A lie can be repeated unchallenged, with scant risk that those whom it reaches will also hear the other side of the story, or be inclined — or, practically, even be able — to test the accuracy or sources for the story.

Today, the marketplace of ideas has become a largely undifferentiated mass which we must either sift through for what we want to hear ourselves or rely on others to perform that task for us. The increasing use of AI and algorithms in digital media is only exacerbating this echo-chamber phenomenon. Social media algorithms are not designed to present users with conflicting views about what they are reading, or to counterbalance the fake with the true. That is left to the users themselves, which presupposes the same unlimited time and interest that the Progressives realized was unrealistic to expect from most or even many voters. As the influential legal professor Cass Sunstein aptly observed, a "system of limitless individual choices, with respect to communications, is not necessarily in the interest of citizenship and self-government." With all of Trump's decrying some imagined "deep state," a real problem today is that social media creates siloed "sheep states."

Today, we must also confront another issue that the Progressives took on in the early nineteenth century: wealthy speakers, corporate actors, and media conglomerates are able to dominate the discourse and drown out other voices in the information marketplace. Elon Musk controls the influential social media network X, giving him the ability to prioritize certain voices and types of information over others. In this sense, the role of folks like Musk and other social media executives today, whether intentional or not, has an effect analogous to that played by Boss Tweed a century ago.

Most dangerous of all to our democracy is that the current social media marketplace permits falsehoods to flourish, with no guarantee that the truth will prevail all or even most of the time. The marketplace can be polluted with propaganda, disinformation, and emotional manipulation. That the Trump administration is fighting efforts to thwart online disinformation, under the guise of defending the First Amendment, exacerbates this problem. In short, authoritarians use the cloak of the freedom of speech to promulgate false factual speech and drown out the truth.

Differentiating the public lie from the private truth is only going to grow harder in the years ahead. As AI experts repeatedly warn, so-called deep fakes are now beginning to allow public liars to cloak falsehoods with the mantle of truth. These technologies allow liars to supercharge their lies, making it that much more difficult for the public to differentiate fact from fiction. Even President Trump appeared fooled by a doctored image of Kilmar Abrego Garcia, one of the many immigrants illegally seized and sent to rot in an El Salvador prison by Trump without due process of law — apparently thinking that the Tren de Aragua gang tattoos superimposed on Abrego Garcia's hands in the image were real.

To make matters worse, truthful government data is also becoming scarcer. When you have a president who seeks to fire and punish truth-tellers, and to sanitize Executive Branch offices of hard data, it is increasingly difficult to frack down to the ground truth underneath the thick crust of lies. Which is precisely the point: the "truth" becomes what the president and his administration say it is, with no hard data to contradict his claims, no matter how robust the news ecosystem might be. Scientists at HHS are removed for advocating the correct science regarding vaccines; the head of the Bureau of Labor Statistics is fired when the numbers are poor; websites are purged of information about historical weather patterns; and employees who speak truth to power are fired, like former DOJ attorney Erez Reuveni who conceded that Abrego Garcia was erroneously removed from this country by the government. (He filed a whistleblower complaint detailing how he was unwilling to lie to the court to cover up failing to follow court orders.) And law firms that might defend these people from illegal retaliation are chilled from doing so by being put on unconstitutional Trump blacklists. None of this makes it any easier for citizens to separate fact from fiction.

I know this all too well from my work for Special Counsel Robert Mueller on the investigation of Russian interference in the 2016 election. His lengthy final report concluded (as did a bipartisan Senate intelligence report) that Russia engaged in an extensive propaganda campaign from the safety of its Internet operations center in Saint Petersburg. The blandly named Internet Research Agency engaged in what it itself described as "information warfare against the United States of America." The agency promoted myriad false stories about Trump's rivals, first in the Republican primary, and then in the general election. It sought to suppress certain likely Democratic voters (posing as American Black voters disillusioned with being sold out by Democrats, for instance). Agency employees were instructed to "use any opportunity to criticize Hilary and the rest (except Sanders and Trump — we support them)." It created numerous fake personas and hundreds of social media accounts to make it appear on social media that the messages were coming from patriotic Americans, not Russian operatives. Lest you think that our findings were biased, a bipartisan Senate Report reached the exact same conclusions, based on hard physical evidence. Then-Senator Marco Rubio was one of the signatories on that report.

That much was cut-and-dried — but when it came to determining whether the Russians were violating any laws, the problem of accountability for political lies reared its head. The Russians could not be charged with simply defrauding the American public due to the same loophole in our legal system that allows Trump to get away with his lies about election fraud. Instead, our team had to see if there were other crimes that we could charge the Russians with. Because there was evidence that the Russian actors had stolen American identities to create fake Internet personas, we could seek charges of identity theft. Because they did not register with the Department of Justice as agents of a foreign government, the indictment alleged they had violated the Foreign Agents Registration Act, which required such registration. But the real harm — the reason the public would care about what they were up to — was the intentional lying to the American electorate to sway their votes, and that did not violate any criminal statute. The consequences for such lying was left to some imagined marketplace of ideas on the Internet to sort itself out before it could affect the election.

We will truly never know what effect the Russian interference had on the 2016 presidential election. If it hadn't happened, Trump may very well still have won. But this hypothetical, while worth pondering, is actually beside the point. We should not have to wonder about this sort of thing in the first place; we should have a legal system that prevents, or at least reduces the risk of, election lies.

The marketplace of ideas is not that system. So what is?

CHAPTER 4

STOLEN VALOR

s there anything we can do to stop politicians from lying about hard facts and to hold them accountable if they do? The short answer is yes. Here, as in so many other domains, the law can help us — if we let it. The field of law is not like the scientific world — a realm my father lived in. In science, nothing we do is going to alter the very existence of gravity, for instance. But in law, we can construct the world as we see fit.

But congressional laws are not written on a blank slate. There are constitutional guardrails that limit what statutes Congress can pass into law: these are the margins within which US statutory laws must be written. In the law school where I teach—indeed, in all law schools—students learn the basic hierarchy of our nation's laws. The federal Constitution is at the top, with congressional statutes subordinated to it. This means that Congress cannot pass a law that violates the Constitution—for instance, a statute may not infringe on the constitutional right to the freedom of speech as established in the First Amendment. This is a fundamental tenet of American law, so any step we take toward regulating by statute the speech of politicians would need to stay on the right side of the Constitution.

This isn't as easy as it may sound. (Welcome to the law—where things can get complicated fast.) In law school, my students learn that the Constitution rarely provides a clear and specific answer to a legal question. In those situations, it's up to the courts to interpret the Constitution's text based on the words in the document itself as well as an amalgam of historical context and practice, plus legal principles and case precedents. A lot of ink has been spilled on arguments about how the courts should engage in this process of divination.

In our system of divided government, the Supreme Court is the ultimate arbiter of how to interpret the Constitution. Its decisions comprise a body of case law that determines these constitutional guardrails. A case might arise if Congress passes a law it believes is within the bounds of the Constitution, but a person affected by that law challenges it after the law is enacted. The lawsuit is asking the courts to determine whether the law in fact passes constitutional muster. The courts are not being asked to decide the wisdom of the law — that is, whether the judges would have enacted the law if they were in Congress — but only whether the law violates the Constitution. Judges are supposed to decide only that issue, even if they find the statute unwise, heinous, or cruel.

In our specific situation, to make matters trickier, the Supreme Court has not directly addressed the issue of how a statute might rein in political lies. As we lawyers like to say, there is no case directly "on point." The closest that the Court has come was in a 2012 case called *United States v. Alvarez.* As we confront the question of how to hold Trump and other politicians to account for lies, this case provides the best guidance about the options before us.

The defendant in this Supreme Court case, Xavier Alvarez, was an elected member of the Three Valleys Water District Board in California. In a public meeting of the board in 2007, Alvarez claimed that he had been awarded the Congressional Medal of Honor, was a retired marine, and a wounded veteran. That was all a lie. In fact, Alvarez had quite a history of telling tall tales: he claimed to have played professional hockey, to have been married to a Mexican starlet, to have served in the marines for twenty-five years, and to have been wounded many times. He said that he had rescued the American ambassador during the Iranian hostage crisis and, in case that show of derring-do was not sufficiently impressive, he allegedly was shot in the back as he returned to the embassy to save the American flag. All were reported lies. As the Supreme Court observed, lying "was his habit."

Alvarez was criminally prosecuted for lying under a specific federal statute, the Stolen Valor Act of 2005. That law made it a misdemeanor for a person to falsely represent "himself or herself, verbally or in writing, to have been awarded any decoration or medal authorized by Congress for the Armed Forces of the United States." The penalty was enhanced from a maximum of six months to a year for a lie about receiving the Medal of Honor.

If you think that Trump's presidential election fraud lie is an outlier, dispel that thought by looking at the honesty crisis that led Congress to enact the Stolen Valor Act. The law was a response to an "epidemic of false claims about military decorations," as one of the Supreme Court Justices who eventually weighed in on the case would put it. In just a single year, over 600 Virginia residents falsely claimed to have won the Medal of Honor. That is just in one year in one state. Of the 333 people who were listed in the online *Who's Who* as having received a top military award, a third could not be substantiated. Anecdotal evidence was no better: a judge claimed to have been awarded not one, but two Medals of Honor, neither of which he had actually received — although he displayed both counterfeits in his courtroom.

Before his trial on the charge that he violated the Stolen Valor Act, Alvarez filed a motion to dismiss the case against him. He argued that the statute violated the First Amendment — exactly what I would have argued, too, if I were his defense counsel. That is the counsel's job: thinking of creative, good-faith arguments in your client's defense. You are required to be their zealous advocate, but always within the bounds of the law and subject to your duty of candor to the courts. You give it your all to provide the client with their right to effective counsel and to hold the government to its burden to establish guilt beyond a reasonable doubt.

Alvarez's counsel did that, but his motion was denied, at least at the initial trial court level. After Alvarez lost the motion, he pleaded guilty instead of going to trial — but he reserved his right to appeal on First Amendment grounds. He did just that, and in February 2012 his appeal made it all the way up to the Supreme Court, giving the Justices the opportunity to decide whether or not the Stolen Valor Act of 2005 violated the First Amendment.

Alvarez and his tenacious defense counsel won in the Supreme Court — but the court's decision found the act unconstitutional on narrow grounds, requiring only slight modifications to the statute going forward. Congress enacted those revisions, and the Stolen Valor Act of 2013, revised to conform to the Supreme Court's decision, is on the books today. But for Alvarez personally that was a huge win, since that new criminal law could not apply retroactively to his conduct.

The *Alvarez* case produced no majority opinion — that is, no opinion that garnered the support of at least five of the nine Supreme Court Justices. As Justice Sandra Day O'Connor famously quipped, "At the end of the day, being on the Supreme Court is about getting to five." None of the three opinions in *Alvarez* got to five. But the reasoning in the three opinions is nonetheless useful for us, because it reveals potential pathways forward as well as potential obstacles to holding politicians to account for lies.

The three different opinions in the *Alvarez* case are the best we have from the Court to guide our thinking about the legality of possible solutions to our current political mess. But one thing is quite clear: because none of the three opinions was able to amass five votes, there is no "holding" that dictates what the law requires. We just have guidance from three sets of Justices, and not even from all the same Justices who are currently serving on the Court today.

In defending the *Alvarez* prosecution, the US government was represented by the government's lead appellate lawyer, the formidable United States Solicitor General Donald Verrilli Jr. (I first met Verrilli when, a year ahead of me at Columbia Law School, he was the editor in chief of the law review. We all knew then he was destined for great things.) He argued that provably false speech serves no First Amendment interest and deserves no protection itself under the Constitution. The government contended that Congress was furthering through this statute the perfectly legitimate goal of protecting the integrity of the Medal of Honor and its actual recipients. After all, Verrilli argued, all the people falsely claiming to have received the medal were cheapening the coin of the realm, and might even arouse unjust suspicion of heroes who actually had won the medal. The statute did not prohibit people from criticizing the military, nor did it limit speech about the awarding of medals in general or of this particular one to any individual recipient.

Six Justices rejected the government's position, for differing reasons, and found that the law violated the First Amendment. Although that sounds like a resounding loss for the government, in reality it was anything but. All six of those Justices signed on to a workaround that salvaged the statute with only minor tweaks. And the three Justices who were in dissent would have upheld the statute as written. So in reality, but for fairly minor changes, the Congressional prohibition of false speech about military medals was sanctioned by all nine of the Justices.

Of the three *Alvarez* opinions, the one authored by (now retired) Justice Anthony Kennedy is the most hostile to the constitutionality of the congressional statute, and it alerts us to some of the biggest potential stumbling blocks for a law governing political speech. The Kennedy opinion was joined by Chief Justice John Roberts and Justices Ruth Bader Ginsburg and Sonia Sotomayor. (The composition of the Court has changed since 2012, and only two of those four Justices are still presiding: Roberts and Sotomayor. A similar changing of the guard affects the potential continued vitality of the other two opinions in *Alvarez*.)

Kennedy's opinion is at core a contradiction, and is best understood by the old adage "what I do makes a mockery of what I say." Kennedy starts by intoning that the way to deal with the false Alvarez claim is "counterspeech." As he explained, "The remedy for speech that is false is speech that is true. This is the ordinary course in a free society." This idea, we know, is an outgrowth of the Holmes "marketplace of ideas." But in the end, Kennedy would uphold a new version of the law that bears an uncanny similarity to the one he voted to strike down.

Kennedy had to concede that Congress had already regulated speech, both civilly and criminally, in innumerable ways that the Supreme Court has blessed. When someone lies to commit fraud or obtain something of value, for instance, "it is well established that the Government may restrict speech without affronting the First Amendment," Kennedy wrote. This is why I was able to prosecute the lies by Kenneth Lay and Jeffrey Skilling under statutes that passed constitutional muster. Defamation and speech integral to criminal conduct are other examples of categories of speech that the First Amendment does not protect, conceded Kennedy. And that is the rubric that permitted Dominion's suit against Fox and the Freeman/Moss case against Giuliani.

Kennedy also had to admit that perjury statutes are similarly of "unquestioned constitutionality." He gave two reasons: perjured statements are by definition false, and perjured testimony is "at war with justice" because it risks a court rendering a "judgment not resting on truth." Perjury thus undermines the function and province of the courts, which "are the basis of the legal system." Kennedy made much the same observations with respect to false representations, although not under oath, when made to federal authorities (the statute at issue in prosecuting Martha Stewart, Paul Manafort, and countless others).

In other words, Kennedy had to concede that the Court had hardly applied the principle consistently that the best antidote to a lie is the truth — the Holmes model. Instead, the law often civilly regulates and even criminalizes false speech.

Kennedy nonetheless was concerned that the position of the government in the *Alvarez* case would open the door to the criminalization of a broad swath of speech, permitting the Government "to compile a list of subjects about which false statements are punishable." This led Kennedy to conclude that where the government was engaged in "content-based speech regulation," the courts needed to subject the regulation to "exacting scrutiny."

While Kennedy professed vigilance, his vaunted "exacting" scrutiny could be met by only minor changes to the Stolen Valor law. The problem with the Stolen Valor Act was only that it was too broad, Kennedy quibbled. For him, the problem with the statute was that it could sweep in other people, speaking in contexts where there was little need for the statute because the harm was minimal, if any. It applied to false statements "at any time, in any place, to any person." Although Xavier Alvarez made his statements in a public forum, the statute applied, technically, to even a whispered private conversation "within a home." Further, the statute did not require that the lie be "made for the purpose of material gain" or "advantage," but covered mere braggadocio. With these tweaks, the bromide about the "antidote" to false speech being truthful speech could seemingly be brushed aside.

Notably for our purposes, the twin sins in the 2005 Stolen Valor Act articulated by Kennedy would not pose an obstacle to a statute regulating election lies. A new law governing political lies could easily avoid the Scylla and Charybdis of the problems that Kennedy identified with the Stolen Valor Act. The political lies we care about are those made to the public and are made for the purpose of electoral advancement. So long as a new law does not regulate purely private speech, and the restricted speech is undertaken for some material gain or advantage, the problems Kennedy identified in *Alvarez* would be inapplicable. Indeed, Kennedy's affirmation in *Alvarez* that Congress has a legitimate interest in regulating perjury applies equally to a congressional statute that would restrict lies that undermine the electoral process, if not more so. It would be professional hubris to differentiate in our constitutional firmament false-statement laws on the grounds that lies affecting a court proceeding are more pernicious than lies affecting a ballot box.

The other two Supreme Court opinions in the *Alvarez* case, although less hostile to the Stolen Valor Act of 2005, are nonetheless important for our purposes. They contain reflections by five other justices about the sorts of speech regulations that they worried about in the future — thereby giving us a clearer picture of the strictures that a law about political lies may need to abide by.

Justice Stephen Breyer — who also has since stepped down from the Court — wrote the second opinion in the *Alvarez* case, an opinion that concurred with Kennedy's, but not for all the same reasons. Justice Elena Kagan was the sole other Justice to sign on to Breyer's opinion, which staked out a middle ground: agreeing with Kennedy's conclusion that the statute was too broad, Breyer applied a more relaxed legal test that gave Congress greater leeway in regulating false speech. Instead of subjecting the Stolen Valor Act to the "exacting" scrutiny applied by Kennedy (what we lawyers generally refer to as "strict scrutiny"), Breyer contended that a lesser standard — "intermediate" scrutiny — was the appropriate test.

It would be fair to ask whether the lower level of review that Breyer advanced was really necessary, given how easy it was for Congress to tweak the statute to meet the "exacting" test set out by Kennedy. Putting that cavil aside, Breyer's middle-ground approach involves a balancing of factors, which are largely common sense dressed up in legal garb. He identifies and weighs various interests: the nature and importance of the Stolen Valor Act's objectives, the extent to which the statute achieves its goals, the direct and indirect First Amendment harms from the statute, and whether there are less harmful ways to achieve Congress's goals. For readers who haven't been to law school, this is a fine example of how there are often competing principles and values at play in a legal case and why it can be difficult for courts to draw a hard and fast line that governs all future cases. Cases are not decided on broad, bold statements of principle but on the balancing of competing values, taking into account the particular facts of the case.

Breyer recognizes the strong governmental interest in banning intentionally false speech about the receipt of military awards. He candidly agrees that such lies are hard to justify as advancing an important discussion of ideas. False factual statements, he writes, are "less likely than true factual statements to make a valuable contribution to the marketplace of ideas." That is why, he noted, the Supreme Court's prior cases "frequently said or implied" that false factual statements enjoy little First Amendment protection. Just a few years earlier, the Court had said that false statements of fact "are particularly valueless." In fact, the Court had gone so far as to say that such statements are "not worthy of constitutional protection."

But Breyer does identify a possible indirect harmful effect of the Stolen Valor Act. Even if the false factual statements themselves are of little or no value, the statute has the potential to chill truthful speech and thus have an impermissible spillover effect. The Stolen Valor Act minimizes that risk, he acknowledges, by only applying to clear and verifiable facts, not the expression of ideas about "philosophy, religion, history, the social sciences, the arts, and the like." As Breyer writes, "The dangers of suppressing valuable ideas are lower where, as here, the regulations concern false statements about easily verifiable facts that do not concern such subject matter." The thought is that, by criminalizing an intentionally false claim about receiving a Medal of Honor, the government would not likely dissuade people from expressing views about other subjects, even ones that are closely related, such as the use, function, or value of the military or its award criteria.

Having explained these reservations, Breyer turns to the concern that, I think, truly animates his concurring opinion — selective prosecution. Breyer worries that, if the

Court permits false statements to be criminalized, it could inadvertently hand a "weapon to a government." He posits that "those who are unpopular" may fear that the government will use the weapon against them, prosecuting false statements only when they come from individuals or organizations that the government disfavors. The statute could lie around like a Chekhovian gun, waiting to be used against political enemies. In "political contexts," the lie might cause even more harm, Breyer rightly observes, risking the "censorious selectivity" of the party in power. Breyer astutely flips the ubiquity of falsehoods on its head, observing that selective prosecution is that much more of a risk given "the pervasiveness of false statements." The prevalence of lies raises the danger that, when the government enforces a law against false statements, it can choose its perceived enemies to target — much as we have witnessed the police in certain locales use everyday traffic violations to selectively target minority groups.

I sympathize completely with Breyer's concerns. The first Trump administration, and the beginning of the second, demonstrate that fears like these are not fanciful or hypothetical. When the executive branch calls for the investigation and prosecution of Democrats, views the Democratic Party as a domestic terrorism threat, and seeks to apply the law more favorably to allies of the president, we know that selective, malicious, and vindictive prosecution is a real issue. Just look at the example of DOJ declining to even investigate "Border Czar" Tom Homan, who was reportedly caught in a sting operation accepting a bag from the Cava fast-food chain containing $50,000 in cash. Or just ask James Comey, whom, in a stretch, the Trump administration sought to indict using the false statement law as its weapon of choice. My own experience during the Mueller investigation exposed me to the example of a "show trial" of a political adversary in Ukraine: that of Yulia Tymoshenko, a political rival of Ukraine president Viktor Yanukovych. Her prosecution was widely condemned by the West as a paradigmatic example of selective prosecution, not solely because of doubt about the reliability of the evidence against her, but because the crime was one that was often violated and rarely enforced.

The problem with Breyer's analysis, though, is that the very real problem of selective prosecution exists whether or not the Stolen Valor Act of 2005 is on the books. Breyer's concern is not specific to the Stolen Valor Act. In the United States, there are thousands of existing criminal laws, including false-statement crimes, which can be weaponized by an unscrupulous president or attorney general. The Stolen Valor Act is just one more statute that can be subject to abuse. None of these laws is constitutionally infirm because they can be abused by a corrupt executive. The statute itself is not illegal; what should be illegal is the manner of implementation by the abuser. The solution to the concern about selective prosecution must be addressed in the legal edifice that the Supreme Court has created to evaluate selective, malicious, and vindictive prosecution claims raised by defendants. That edifice is virtually impregnable, and in need of reform.

As for Breyer's point that lies are quotidian (and thus that statutes addressing lies are susceptible to being weaponized), that hardly translates to concluding that we should not subject lies to any regulation at all. Should we also stop regulating crimes once we decide that they're too commonly committed? To argue the same about political lies would be astounding: it would mean we should not only expect them, but also condone them. Prevalence is a reason to take action, not to stand down.

Breyer did not address a related problem to that of selective prosecution, but it is worth flagging. What if the party in power seeks to hold a member of an opposing party liable for a true statement under the guise of it being false? There would be an almost unlimited number of such statements that a corrupt administration could choose to go after. Fortunately, the criminal legal system is designed to deal with exactly this issue. There are a variety of built-in checks that, together, serve to restrain a dominant party from successfully prosecuting its rivals. Department of Justice lawyers could balk (a barrier that traditionally has worked, but has proven to be porous). Grand jurors (made up of everyday citizens) could refuse to indict the government's target for a lack of probable cause. We have witnessed this repeatedly in the second Trump administration, even though the phenomenon is simply unheard of in normal Republican or Democratic administrations. A trial jury (similarly composed) could acquit the person on the ground that the crime had not been proved beyond a reasonable doubt, and the courts could throw out a guilty verdict as unsupported by the weight of the evidence.

Systemic checks such as these are only a partial safeguard against this danger, however — because even if they all work, a person so targeted would be subject to an expensive and time-consuming investigation and possible trial. Again, just ask James Comey about this possibility. The mere threat of such an improper investigation and prosecution, moreover, could serve to chill speech — which, under Trump, I would argue, is rapidly happening already.

This nightmare scenario is why the Department of Justice has an internal rule embodied in its *Justice Manual* that, as a matter of "fundamental fairness," no prosecution "should be initiated against any person unless the attorney for the government believes that the admissible evidence is sufficient to obtain and sustain a guilty verdict by an unbiased trier of fact." This provision exists to prevent a person from facing charges when the government has insufficient reason to believe it will obtain a valid conviction at trial and be able to sustain it on appeal. In my experience, this rule (which is a norm, not an enforceable law) was followed in every other Democratic and Republican administration for which I worked. It serves to prevent the situation that seemed clearly to be at play in the Letitia James and James Comey cases: even if the government meets the low standard of probable cause to obtain a grand jury indictment, it is not supposed to subject a person to charges unless it has a sufficient basis to believe it can satisfy the much higher burden at trial of proof beyond a reasonable doubt found by a unanimous jury.

The Supreme Court Justices who signed the third opinion in the *Alvarez* case dissented from the conclusion that the law violated the First Amendment, but despite that assessment they made observations that are pertinent to regulating political lies. Justice Samuel Alito wrote the dissent, joined by Justices Clarence Thomas and Antonin Scalia, the latter of whom has since passed away.

Alito's opinion praises, rightly, the military and the award system. "Only the bravest of the brave are awarded the Congressional Medal of Honor," he writes in the bracing opening line of the dissent, "but the Court today holds that every American has a constitutional right to claim to have received this singular award." In high dudgeon, he goes on to ask whether it was reasonable for Congress to conclude that the goal of preserving the integrity of military honors was worthy of the same protection that the law provides to thwart counterfeiting "fancy watches and designer handbags." Trademark law protects genuine luxury items from the proliferation of knockoffs. Are military honors, Alito acidly asks, no less worthy of such protection?

Alito denigrates Kennedy's view that, for the Stolen Valor Act to not be impermissibly overbroad, the statute needed to require that the lie about being awarded a military honor must have "caused specific harm." For Alito, all such lies cause damage to actual award recipients and to the military honor system. In another rhetorical takedown, Alito observes that, "unless even a small financial loss — say, a dollar given to a homeless man falsely claiming to be a decorated veteran — is more important in the eyes of the First Amendment than the damage caused to the very integrity of the military awards system, there is no basis for distinguishing between the Stolen Valor Act and the alternative statutes that the plurality and concurrence appear willing to sustain." Alito compares the sorts of lies that the Stolen Valor Act penalizes to the crime of making a false statement to the government, which the Supreme Court had previously decided was constitutional even without a showing of either a property loss to the government or a benefit to the prevaricator. The Court held that the false-statement law was constitutional because it fulfilled the need to protect the government from the "perversion which might result from the deceptive practices." So, too, with the Stolen Valor Act, as Alito cogently observed.

But in his dissent, Alito in fact goes out of his way to acknowledge that criminalizing lies can pose First

Amendment problems. Although he believes false statements of fact do not merit First Amendment protection "for their own sake," he recognizes that it is necessary to extend a measure of "strategic protection" to ensure "breathing space for protected speech." In other words, he agrees with the other Justices that protection for false speech may be necessary so as not to chill truthful speech on matters of public concern. Alito specifically warns against laws restricting false statements about areas such as philosophy, religion, history, and the social sciences. Such regulation would, in his view, "present a grave and unacceptable danger of suppressing truthful speech." He worries about this not because there is "no such thing as truth or falsity" or that "truth is always impossible to ascertain." Rather, he fears the consequences of allowing the state to be the "arbiter of truth." As an illustration, he asks whether, if some false statements about historical events can be banned, "how certain must it be that a statement is false before the ban may be upheld?" And who, he asks, should make that calculation? Like the other Justices, Alito worries that even if the Stolen Valor Act is worthy, the court needed to be wary lest it "opens the door for the state to use its power for political ends."

Despite these legitimate questions, Congress's response to the *Alvarez* decision — the 2013 version of the Stolen Valor Act — is on the books and is being enforced today. The law criminalizes false claims about military honors, but only if made "with intent to obtain money, property, or other tangible benefit." Not all public lies about military awards fall within the reach of the amended statute, and the newer version of the law is even less likely to be applied to private communications. (Ironically, Xavier Alvarez — although exempt from being retried on the revised statute — may have met these additional requirements if he'd been prosecuted under the new version of the law, because there was a factual basis for the government to claim that at least some of his false statements were made in order to "fraudulently obtain certain benefits.")

The Department of Justice has already brought criminal cases under the improved Stolen Valor Act of 2013. In one case, defendant Randall J. Montour, presumably to increase his employment prospects, falsified his military discharge certificate to reflect that he received an honorable discharge and that he had earned numerous Air Force decorations, including a Purple Heart. To add insult to injury, he applied for and received a special Purple Heart Recipient license plate for his car. In fact, he was not honorably discharged and did not receive a Purple Heart. In another prosecution, defendant Derek Robert Hamm held himself out to be a former Army Special Forces member who had "served multiple tours of duty in Iraq, Afghanistan," and other countries. He boasted to have received not just one, but multiple military medals: the Purple Heart, Bronze Star, Silver Star, and Distinguished Service

Cross. This decorated persona was used by Hamm to woo investors. But as you may have guessed already: all of this was false. As described by the courts, Derek Hamm was cut from the same cloth as that worn by Xavier Alvarez. He may have thought, *Go big or go home*; but now home is jail. He was prosecuted for violating the 2013 statute (among his other crimes) and was sentenced to eleven years in jail.

These challenges to the improved 2013 version of the Stolen Valor Act have all been rejected. No legal challenge has reached the Supreme Court, but if one does it is exceedingly unlikely to succeed, given the limited nature of the flaws in the 2005 law identified in *Alvarez* and the revisions to the law that plugged those gaps.

For anyone hoping to prevent Donald Trump and any other politicians from continuing to damage American democracy with their lies, the precedent set in *Alvarez* makes clear that the Constitution does not put false statements beyond all reach of congressional regulation. This means that we the people — acting through our congressional representatives — may be able to enact laws to curb them, if we choose. And although those laws would surely be challenged in court, they may withstand scrutiny if they were to reach the Supreme Court, so long as their scope — and their impact on true speech — is limited.

So how, exactly, do we strike that balance? How do we construct a law that would protect free speech while also holding politicians accountable?

These are important questions. Fortunately, we're not alone in asking and answering them. Other nations have confronted the threat of political lies, too — and unlike the United States, they have managed to tackle them directly. Other democratic societies are ahead of us in trying to deal with the problem of political falsehoods while staying true to their constitutions, and they have done so in a variety of ways. As our own democracy is stumbling in the dark, these examples light various paths forward.

CHAPTER 5

LOOKING OVERSEAS

We rarely look outside our country for guidance. This American aversion may emanate from our being geographically cut off from much of the world, or it may stem from a belief in our exceptionalism or its uglier companion, xenophobia. Whatever the reason, we are the ones who lose out when we ignore other nations' solutions to problems that we, too, are confronting. We deprive ourselves of the chance to learn about new tools that could help us fortify our democracy.

Don't just take it from me. Supreme Court Justice Ruth Bader Ginsburg believed that, just as our American experience may be instructive to foreign nations, "so too can we learn from others" whose courts have sought to measure governmental actions against their countries' constitutional rights. We may not always agree with other countries' solutions to challenges like the ones we're facing, and we might not always find them apposite given the differences in our countries' unique histories and legal and political systems. But that doesn't justify our ignoring whatever lessons they might hold out of a misguided sense of self-worth, laziness, or nativism.

When it comes to the threat of political lies, the lessons are especially rich and instructive. Several countries have devised innovative ways to deal with this problem. Brazil, France, and Germany offer three useful models of how to deal with lies. Each of their systems is different, yet all strike a balance — similar to the one that the Supreme Court demanded in the *Alvarez* case — between thwarting lies and maintaining robust protections for people's basic rights, including the right of free speech. As we consider how to hold American politicians accountable for deceit without abandoning our own fierce attachment to the First Amendment, it's illuminating to consider how these three countries have navigated the same basic tension.

THE BRAZILIAN EXAMPLE

One sign that Brazil has a particularly effective solution to the challenge of political lies is that Donald Trump has taken serious issue with it — at least, when that strategy has been applied to the political lies of Brazil's former president, Jair Bolsonaro. Trump is uncannily reflected in Bolsonaro's actions. So it's to Brazil, and Bolsonaro, that we turn first.

Before running for president in 2018, Jair Bolsonaro spent nearly three decades representing Rio de Janeiro in the Brazilian Congress, where he championed nationalism and social conservatism. He made repeated inflammatory statements about women, minorities, and democracy. He is reported to have said to a congresswoman that he would not rape her because "she doesn't deserve it because she's very ugly. She's not my type." He reportedly said that voting in Brazilian elections wouldn't give his followers the changes they sought; rather, he claimed, things would change "the day we begin a civil war," even if "some innocents will die." Brazil's congress didn't work, he claimed, so "let's do the coup, already."

Despite all of his disparaging statements about the country's electoral system, he announced his candidacy for president in July 2018; two months later, a man stabbed Bolsonaro in the stomach during a rally, but he recovered, continued campaigning, and maintained his lead in the polls. In a decisive victory, Bolsonaro was elected president of Brazil in October 2018. During his presidency, he continued in the same vein as his tenure in the National Congress, continuing to attack democratic institutions and the Brazilian electoral system.

Bolsonaro's reign came to an end in 2022, when he ran for reelection and lost. Not long after, on January 8, 2023, about 5,000 Bolsonaro supporters stormed key government buildings in the country's capital, Brasilia, including the National Congress. Once inside, they vandalized chambers, broke windows, and assaulted numerous police officers. The rioters were driven by false claims of election fraud in the 2022 presidential election, alleged skullduggery that they believed had resulted in Bolsonaro's wrongful defeat. Over 1,400 people would eventually face criminal charges for their actions that day, with key participants receiving double-digit jail sentences.

It is hard not to see Jair Bolsonaro as a Brazilian version of Donald Trump, up to and including the attempted insurrections in their names and their belittling the seriousness of sexual assault on women. In fact, in both countries, these two men were successfully sued in civil court by the respective women they vilified. The comparison between the two politicians ends, however, with the legal ramifications of their election lies.

Brazil, unlike the United States, prohibits intentionally lying about the presidential electoral system. Article 22 of Brazil's Complementary Law No. 64 prohibits "the misuse, diversion, or abuse of economic power or the power of authority, or the improper use of vehicles or means of social communication, for the benefit of a candidate or political party." Article 23 further provides that the "Court shall form its conviction through the free assessment of public and notorious facts, indications and presumptions, and evidence produced, paying attention to circumstances or facts, even if not indicated or alleged by the parties, but which preserve the public interest of electoral integrity."

If a person is found to have violated either of these statutes, Brazilian law disqualifies them from running for office for a set period of time. This sanction was authorized under a separate law colloquially known as the *Ficha Limpa* or "Clean Slate Law." The 2010 law came about after intense and effective work by civil society groups, nonprofits, and religious organizations, including the collection of a reported three million signatures on petitions seeking election reform.

The Clean Slate Law amended Complementary Law No. 64 by specifying that a conviction for "abuse of political power" or "misuse of media" during electoral campaigns triggers a mandatory disqualification period:

Holders of positions in...public administration who benefit themselves or third parties through the abuse of economic or political power, and who are convicted in a final and unappealable decision or a decision rendered by a collegiate judicial body, are ineligible for the election in which they are running or have been certified, as well as for those held in the following [eight] years.

Brazil's legal model rests on the premise that the right to truthful information in elections supersedes an unfettered right to free speech when deliberate falsehoods are made that threaten the democratic order. Think of it as a "truth in advertising" law, but transplanted from the realm of consumer protection to the sphere of voter protection and election integrity. This principle is enshrined in the Brazilian Electoral Code and has been upheld and reinforced by judicial rulings, reflecting a societal consensus about the dangers of disinformation.

To be sure, the application of the Clean Slate Law to a Brazilian president was historic. But this did not prevent the country from seeing Bolsonaro charged. His trial was not inordinately delayed by the courts, nor was he protected by presidential immunity. Instead, he was afforded due process, tried in court, and found liable.

The trial of Bolsonaro before the Tribunal Superior Eleitoral, commonly referred to as the TSE, was for two charges of knowingly making false statements designed to sow public distrust in the electoral process, in direct contravention of article 22 of Complementary Law no. 64. Just as in the United States, these laws require the prosecution to establish that the defendant's statements were not merely false, but were intentionally so — what we refer to as the defendant's *mens rea*, or mental state. The law does not prohibit statements if they are made in the good-faith, but erroneous, belief that the election was infected by fraud.

The trial produced irrefutable evidence that Bolsonaro had persistently and publicly claimed that Brazil's electronic voting system was compromised by fraud. It also established beyond a doubt the accuracy and reliability of Brazil's electronic voting machines (just as the US judge in the Dominion case found, with respect to that company's voting machines). Independent technical experts submitted detailed reports verifying that the machines functioned transparently and without material risk of fraud, despite Bolsonaro's claims to the contrary.

The court also was presented with strong evidence that demonstrated Bolsonaro's intent—showing that he did not believe his own claims about election tampering. The court found that, in spite of Bolsonaro's knowing that election officials and repeated audits had found no fraud that affected the election results, he repeatedly claimed otherwise and did so in public settings in order to undermine confidence in the election and to inflame his supporters.

In a verdict delivered by five of the TSE's seven judges, the court found Bolsonaro liable. The majority opinion, authored by Justice Benedito Gonçalves, meticulously dissected Bolsonaro's claims. The court found that he had, with full knowledge that he was lying, disseminated "disinformation for electoral purposes" in violation of the Brazilian statutes. Justice Gonçalves emphasized that Bolsonaro's actions transcended mere political rhetoric:

There was an abuse of political power, practiced personally by Jair Messias Bolsonaro, who…used his position as President of the Republic, Head of State, and "supreme commander" of the Armed Forces to enhance the effects of the massive disinformation campaign regarding the Brazilian elections presented to the international community and the electorate.

The court's decision linked Bolsonaro's campaign of disinformation to the physical attacks by mobs on Brazil's Congress and its Supreme Court, drawing a direct connection between the attacks and the public's erosion of faith in the electoral process — a mistrust that the president's lies had fomented.

The penalty that the court handed down to Bolsonaro entailed no prison time or even a fine, but it was significant nevertheless. The TSE judges imposed an eight-year ineligibility sanction on Bolsonaro, barring him from seeking or holding public office through October 2030. Two aggravating factors supported the eight-year bar: the election lies were about the highest office in the land, and they were promulgated by the person holding that highest office. The import of this penalty was clear, and it sent a potent message: in Brazil, intentionally spreading disinformation about the electoral system will be met with serious legal consequences.

The Brazilian legal system was not finished with Bolsonaro. Like the United States, the country has a criminal law against participating in a coup. And like Donald Trump, Bolsonaro was criminally charged with that separate offense. But unlike Trump, Bolsonaro's case actually went to trial.

Before the Brazilian judges issued their verdict in that second Bolsonaro case, Trump (now president in his second term in office) publicly attacked Brazil and the lead judge. He issued a 50 percent tariff on the country and personal sanctions against the judges. Not one for subtlety, Trump gave as the reason for the tariffs not economics (the stated reason for all the other Trump tariffs), but the court's treatment of Bolsonaro. In a letter to the Brazilian president, Trump said he greatly respected Bolsonaro and, using one of his go-to epithets, decried the treatment of Bolsonaro as a "Witch Hunt" and "international disgrace." The American president cited no facts to support those claims.

Undeterred and unbowed, four of the five judges voted to convict Bolsonaro. He was sentenced to twenty-seven years and three months in jail. Trump decried the sentence as "terrible" and "bad for Brazil." The Brazilian president, Luiz Inácio Lula da Silva, had none of it, responding that "no one is above the law." He added, perhaps too optimistically, that the "world has changed. We don't want an emperor."

* * *

In anticipation of the America First crowd dismissing this Brazil model as emanating from a country it looks down on, I'll note that the United Kingdom, too, has a longstanding law to the same effect. The British impose the remedy of disqualification for certain election lies, although they have rarely had to resort to implementing this law.

Originally passed by Parliament in 1895, the British law provides that, whether "before or during an election" a person shall be guilty if, "for the purpose of affecting" the election, the person makes "any false statement of fact in relation to a candidate's personal character or conduct" unless the person can show that they had a reasonable basis for believing the statement and did in fact believe it. The law is now embodied in the UK's Representation of the People Act 1983.

In 2010, the British courts stripped a politician named Philip Woolas of his general election victory in a race for a seat in the House of Commons for falsely accusing his opponent, Robert Watkins, of condoning extreme violence, including the murder of Woolas. Woolas appealed, arguing that his freedom of speech had been violated, but a court rejected his appeal on the basis that the law only applied to false speech, which was not entitled to such protection. "The right to freedom of expression under Article 10 [of the Human Rights Convention relating to freedom of speech] does not extend to a right to be dishonest and tell lies, but [the People Act 1983] is more limited in its scope as it refers to false statements made in relation to a candidate's personal character or conduct." The Election Court ordered a new election, and Woolas was the first MP to be stripped of his election to the House of Commons in nearly 100 years.

THE FRENCH EXAMPLE

Lest you think that Brazil and the United Kingdom are outliers in restricting their people's eligibility to run for office, look across the water to France. There, Marine Le Pen, the unsettlingly popular far-right French politician, is currently barred from holding elected office for five years. Her crime wasn't lying, but rather embezzlement — yet as we seek to address America's honesty crisis, France has something to teach us, too.

Under French law, a criminal conviction for certain offenses — including violent crimes, fraud, and electoral offenses — can carry the additional penalty of being barred from running for office for up to ten years. In Marine Le Pen's case, she and her conspirators were convicted in March 2025 of embezzling millions of euros, one of the eligible crimes for disqualification. She is appealing her criminal conviction as of this writing, but the court determined that in the meantime, given the severity of the crime, the five-year ban on her running for office remains in effect.

This French model is particularly interesting because many of our American states have similar laws (more on which momentarily), and also because France is a country that even Donald Trump grudgingly respects: a so-called first-world country, and not — in his insulting lexicon — a "shithole." So what lessons does France have to teach the United States about how to hold liars, in particular, to account when they spread their falsehoods on our nation's highest stage?

The Le Pen case is different from Bolsonaro's in many respects — including, of course, the fact that the conduct the court penalized was not, in her case, intentionally false speech about elections. But like Brazil, France criminalizes false speech intended to affect an election, and this crime can be punishable by debarment — specifically, a prohibition on the offender running for public office for a set period of time. France's Electoral Code Article L97 makes it a crime for someone, by "means of false news" or "other fraudulent maneuvers," to sway or divert votes or induce "one or more voters to abstain from voting." France is also like Brazil in that it does not shy away from holding its former political leaders to account criminally. Former French president Nicolas Sarkozy has been convicted, after full trials, not once, but three times for a host of serious offenses.

The French system provides an answer to one of the most frequent questions I get asked, particularly after

Trump was convicted of thirty-four felonies under the laws of the State of New York. People want to know how Trump could be eligible to hold elected office when a convicted felon cannot even vote in an election in many states in our country. In other words, if a felon like Trump could not vote, how can it be lawful for a felon like Trump to run for office? This question is particularly relevant to our search for a remedy for political lies, because the state crimes that resulted in Trump's conviction emanated from his scheme to defraud the electorate in the run-up to the 2016 election. The trial produced convincing evidence that, with the assistance of the *National Enquirer*, Trump was involved in a plot to plant false stories about his political rivals and to "catch and kill" derogatory stories about himself.

So why could Trump still run for federal office after he'd been convicted in this case? The answer is that, unlike France, and unlike most of our fifty states, the United States generally does not have a federal law that disenfranchises someone from running for office upon conviction of a crime. Many individual states do impose disqualification upon convictions for state crimes such as fraud, perjury, and other crimes of moral turpitude, prohibiting either permanently or temporarily someone who has been convicted of one of these crimes from holding public office in that state. But a state law cannot prohibit a person from holding federal office.

I say that our federal laws "generally" do not disenfranchise a person from holding federal office because there is a federal law that imposes debarment as a consequence of conviction. The United States Constitution was amended after the Civil War to provide that if a person engages in insurrection or rebellion, after having taken an oath of office, the person is thereafter ineligible to hold federal office (unless Congress votes a dispensation for him). Section 3 of the Fourteenth Amendment states:

> No person shall…hold any office, civil or military, under the United States, or under any State, who, having previously taken an oath…to support the Constitution of the United States, shall have engaged in insurrection or rebellion against the same, or given aid or comfort to the enemies thereof.

This provision of the Constitution spawned a much-watched legal case in the 2024 presidential campaign. The issue arose as to whether a state could implement this provision to bar a candidate from running for federal office, or whether it had to be implemented federally. Six months before the March 2024 Colorado presidential primary, four Republicans and two unaffiliated Colorado voters filed a petition seeking to disqualify Trump from running for president again. At a trial in

Colorado state court, they introduced evidence that Trump "disrupted the peaceful transfer of power" by intentionally organizing and inciting the crowd that breached the Capitol as Congress was meeting to certify the election results on January 6, 2021. They argued that the constitutional provision applied to Trump because, after taking the presidential oath in 2017, he intentionally incited the breaching of the Capitol on January 6 in order to retain power. They argued that the Colorado secretary of state was required to remove him from that state's primary ballot, noting the Constitution's use of the proscriptive language "[n]o person shall."

The Colorado state courts ruled in favor of the plaintiffs, after the trial court held a hearing and concluded that Trump had fomented an insurrection. This factual finding was consistent with the federal conclusion by a majority of both houses of Congress during the second impeachment process. On January 13, 2021, a majority of the House voted to impeach Trump on this very ground, including his disseminating false claims about election fraud. Although the Senate did not convict Trump by the required two-thirds vote, a majority of fifty-seven senators voted to convict, including seven Republicans.

The Colorado state courts that ruled against Trump did not have the last word on the legal issue, however. The case went up to the US Supreme Court, which reversed the lower courts' decisions unanimously. The decision made sense: only the federal government could disqualify a person from federal office. A state could establish laws governing disqualification of a person from its own state offices — something that most states actually do. But a state is not free to implement the federal Constitution as to those seeking federal office: that is up to the federal government and has to be determined at a national level, so as not to have a patchwork of decisions in the fifty states. "Nothing in the Constitution," the Supreme Court Justices inveighed, "delegates to the States any power to enforce Section 3 against federal officeholders and candidates."

But although the Supreme Court closed the door on the Colorado ruling, it left the window open for federal action. In their decision, the Justices observed that the disqualification "penalty" in Section 3 is "preventive and severe," but notably they did not find it improper. The Court voiced no issue with the penalty of disqualification for insurrection or rebellion. It is in the Constitution, after all.

The Court also observed that both Congress and the states had, historically, made use of the Fourteenth Amendment's debarment penalty. Congress, shortly after ratification of the amendment, passed the Enforcement Act of 1870, a law authorizing federal district attorneys to bring civil actions in federal court to remove anyone holding certain offices — federal or state — in violation of Section 3 of the new constitutional amendment. In addition, Congress passed a criminal statute implementing and expanding on the amendment, 18 U.S.C. § 2383. That law is still on the books. It provides that:

> Whoever incites, sets on foot, assists, or engages in any rebellion or insurrection against the authority of the United States or the laws thereof, or gives aid or comfort thereto, shall be fined under this title or imprisoned not more than ten years, or both; *and shall be incapable of holding any office under the United States.*

Neither of these two statutes was used to prosecute Trump federally. The civil law, the Enforcement Act of 1870, was repealed in 1948 in a general reorganization of the law, apparently jettisoned due to disuse. And disuse also largely explains why the criminal statute, section 2383, was not charged by Special Counsel Jack Smith in his investigation of Donald Trump's attempts to overturn the results of the 2020 presidential election. The statute has simply not been used, as far as anyone is aware of, to prosecute anyone.

Put yourself in the special counsel's shoes for a moment. It was controversial enough for Smith to seek to charge a former president with a crime. If he had chosen to do so using a statute that had never been tested in any reported case, it would have taken the controversy to a whole new level — especially given that Trump's ability to run in the 2024 election hung in the balance. (Of course, it's not hard to come up with retorts to those qualms. We have never before had a former president whom a grand jury, with good reason, charged with acts that fomented an insurrection. This unique criminal activity may well have supported a unique usage of the law.)

In his final report, Smith recites additional reasons for not charging Trump under section 2383, including the lack of legal precedent for what constitutes an "insurrection" for purposes of this criminal statute, and whether seeking to remain in office would qualify. Smith noted that he had available other tried and tested criminal statutes, so there was little need in his view to venture into uncharted and controversial territory.

Whether this was a missed opportunity or not, the fact remains: we have at both the federal and state level examples that follow the French model barring people convicted of certain crimes from running for office.

THE GERMAN EXAMPLE

Germany has a very different model than either Brazil or France. German law forbids a specific topic of speech: the public denial of the existence of the Holocaust. Other European countries have done this as well, but Germany's unique role in the Holocaust makes its legal solution to this problem particularly instructive. Imagine, as a very rough analogy, a law in the United States that prohibited denying the 2020 election was the result of fraud — that is, a law that prohibited false speech on a specific topic.

Whereas Brazil imposes the sanction of disqualification for certain lies, Germany flat out prohibits certain lies. As such, Germany's Holocaust denial law represents a far greater intrusion on people's freedom of speech. Yet the German courts have upheld the Holocaust denial law against legal challenge, even though the German constitution has robust protections for freedom of speech. The initial German court's reasoning is particularly useful for us as we continue searching for models in our own fight against political lies. None other than Justice Ruth Bader Ginsburg singled out the German constitutional court as a "paradigm" of constitutional review as a "safeguard against oppressive government and stirred-up majorities." So looking at how Germany has justified restricting certain sorts of false speech might hold lessons about how we might fashion a just law in the United States.

The German Holocaust denial law provides:

whoever publicly or in an assembly approves of, denies, or downplays an act committed under the rule of National Socialism...in a manner that is liable to cause a disturbance of the public peace, incurs a penalty of imprisonment for a term not exceeding five years or a fine.

The German law solves for two flaws identified by the United States Supreme Court in *Alvarez* in the Stolen Valor Act of 2005. Recall that, in *Alvarez*, the court criticized the Stolen Valor Act of 2005 for being applicable even to private communications in which someone falsely whispers to another to be a military medal recipient. The German law, by contrast, requires the Holocaust denial to be made in public or an "assembly" (meaning a large public or private gathering) in order for the statement to be prohibited by the law. Further, the German law requires that any harm from the regulated speech — that is, the Holocaust denial — must be liable to result in a "disturbance of the public peace." This would exempt immaterial private speech that would not be of a type to result in disruption.

The US Congress used similar, although not identical, language when it amended the Stolen Valor Act in 2013 in light of the *Alvarez* decision. To address the *Alvarez* concerns, Congress added a requirement to the law that the false military award claim be made with the intent to obtain money, property, or other tangible benefit. In doing so, Congress satisfied the Justices' concerns. But the difference in the interests that the United States and Germany chose to protect is telling. Germany's legal system is concerned about protecting public safety (the "public peace"), whereas the United States is oriented toward safeguarding private property ("money, property, or other tangible benefit").

The differences notwithstanding, the German Holocaust denial law is a perfect illustration of why US lawmakers (and the attorneys who advise them) would be wise to be less insular. Our legal system rarely stops to consider what we could learn from other countries that have wrestled with similar issues and may have come up with alternative, and perhaps wiser, ways to solve a shared problem. In the case of the Stolen Valor Act, the original law was passed in 2005, more than a decade after the 1994 German Holocaust denial law. Congress clearly did not apply the lessons from the 1994 German law to the 2005 statute. If they had, they might have incorporated into the Stolen Valor Act the German law's limitations on its law, so that it did not prohibit private and immaterial speech. Such a law would have reduced the risk of violating a person's US First Amendment rights and therefore would have better withstood Xavier Alvarez's constitutional challenge, which in turn would have saved Congress having to amend the statute in 2013.

Thanks in part to its more limited reach, the German Holocaust denial law has weathered a constitutional challenge similar to the one that toppled the original Stolen Valor Act. The challenge came from a far-right German group, the National Democratic Party of Germany (the NPD), which had invited British Holocaust denier David Irving to speak at an upcoming gathering in Munich. There, Irving reportedly was planning to claim that the mass extermination of Jews during the Third Reich never happened. The Munich local government caught wind of this, and permitted the NPD meeting to proceed but forbade advocacy of the "Auschwitz Lie," a term used in Germany to refer to Holocaust denial. The NPD sued, alleging a violation of its free speech rights protected by the German constitution, and the German constitutional court heard the case.

In words that could well have been written by our own Supreme Court, the German court began by differentiating opinions from facts. Opinions, the court observed, are different than facts because "they cannot be proven true or false." Freedom of expression, it went on, relates to the "formation of opinion." The court defined opinions broadly: They are entitled to protection, regardless of whether they are "well-founded or deemed emotional or rational, valuable or worthless, dangerous or harmless."

Statements of fact, on the other hand, are cut from an entirely different cloth — and, according to the German court, ought to be held to a higher legal standard. Unlike opinions, statements of fact "are subject to verification of their truthfulness," the court wrote. In words that again could have come directly from many of the Supreme Court Justices in the *Alvarez* case, the court said that false information itself "does not constitute an interest worthy of protection."

The German court candidly noted that separating a tangled question of opinion and fact could be difficult. Where trying to pull them apart would distort the meaning of the utterance, free speech should protect the statement, it concluded. Statements that blur the lines between opinion and fact ought to enjoy legal protection, such as a judgment as to the level of guilt or responsibility for historical events, which are "complex evaluations not reducible to representations of fact."

Here, too, readers will see an enormous similarity to *Alvarez*, where all of the Justices (including the three in dissent) expressed a concern about the potential "chilling" effect on protected speech that could result from prohibiting intentionally false speech, even if the latter was not itself entitled to protection. Like our Supreme Court in *Alvarez*, moreover, the German court also looked to defamation law for examples of how the law balanced the right of free speech with the rights of people affected by that speech. "When expressions of opinion are seen as a formal insult or vilification," the court found, "protection of personality rights normally comes before freedom of expression."

When the German court refers to freedom of expression — one of several rights protected under the German constitution — the idea is readily familiar to us. So, too, are the concepts in the German constitution of equality before the law, religious liberty, and freedom of assembly and association. German law, using its own unique nomenclature, also explicitly recognizes rights not found in the US Constitution: the inviolability of human dignity; the rights to life, physical integrity, and the development of one's "personality"; the rights to education, to occupation, and to privacy of posts and telecommunications. Those various rights may seem unclear in their meaning and application, but that same could be said of the rights enshrined in the US Bill of Rights. The role of the courts in both nations is to determine both the contours of these rights, and what to do when they rub up against each other in conflicting ways.

Applying these constitutionally protected rights to the specific facts of the Holocaust denial case, the German court found the prohibited utterance — the Holocaust claim that David Irving had been prevented from making when the event where he was scheduled to speak was canceled — to be "demonstrably untrue" in the light of innumerable eyewitness accounts, documents, findings of courts in numerous criminal cases, and historical analysis.

On a recent visit to Germany, I met with a judge who had worked on the court's decision. He reminded me of the importance of one particular part of that case: the court was not dealing with allegations that were still legitimately unsettled. These were established facts; there was both voluminous evidence of the facts and judicial cases resolving the facts, all existing beyond question at the time the David Irving speech at the NPD meeting was prohibited. I could not help thinking that the same thing could be said about Trump's continued assertions that the American electoral system was riddled with fraud: there was clear evidence to refute that idea, no evidence ever produced to support it, and numerous court cases rejecting it.

In the NPD case, moreover, the court was also swayed by the harm that the false speech — that is, Irving's erroneous denial of the Holocaust — would cause to the dignity of the victims of the Holocaust. The false Holocaust denial speech violated the right to human dignity protected under the German constitution. In poignant language, the court noted:

The historical fact that human beings were singled out according to the criteria of the so-called "Nuremberg Laws" and robbed of their individuality for the purpose of extermination puts Jews living in the Federal Republic [of Germany] in a special, personal relationship *vis-à-vis* their fellow citizens; what happened then is also present in this relationship today. It is part of their personal self-perception to be understood as part of a group of people who stand out by virtue of their fate and in relation to whom there is a special moral responsibility on the part of all others and that this is part of their dignity. Respect for this self-perception, for each individual, is one of the guarantees against repetition of this kind of discrimination and forms a basic condition of their lives in the Federal Republic...For the person concerned, this is continuing discrimination against the group to which he or she belongs and, as part of the group, against him or her.

That reasoning, steeped in history and psychology, could unfortunately apply to many groups throughout history. I cannot help but think of our Supreme Court's articulation of the harms of the "separate but equal" doctrine rejected in *Brown v. Board of Education*: to separate Black children "solely because of their race generates a feeling of inferiority as to their status in the community that may affect their hearts and minds in a way unlikely ever to be undone." The same could be said of anyone who is discriminated against because of their race, sex, religion, national origin, or choice of whom they love.

But although its reasoning might resonate with an American reader, the court in the NPD case was operating within a different legal and political environment than the one we find ourselves in, today, here in the United States. The same could be said of the courts in the examples that we've considered above from France and Brazil. All three countries present distinct models for contending with the problem of political lies: Brazil disqualifies a person from holding office if found liable for election lies, something that the UK provides for as well. France disqualifies a person who has been convicted of certain crimes — crimes that go far beyond just crimes involving false speech. Germany prohibits speech on a specific topic if it could affect public safety.

Can we take a page from these countries' playbooks as we try to improve the resiliency of our electoral system? To turn the question on its head: Are we doomed to live in a country whose leaders can lie to the electorate with impunity, or is there something that we can do about it? As we've just seen, foreign democracies offer models that can provide inspiration and hope. But would any of their solutions to the problem of false speech withstand legal scrutiny in the United States, given our Constitution and the *Alvarez* decision? Could they pass First Amendment muster? And if they could, which of them holds the most promise for rescuing our democracy from the ongoing threat of political lies?

Whatever tools we choose, these foreign countries already provide us with an important lesson: a willingness to use the legal solutions at their disposal to hold people to account. Foreign countries have held real trials of their political leaders, not show trials. We have, with the exception of one New York criminal court, failed to do the same. A new Congress can create improvements to our US systems, but it will be for naught if these tools atrophy from disuse.

Napoleon Bonaparte was thought to have remarked that "the tools belong to the man who can use them." As we confront the urgent question of what to do about Donald Trump and his lies, this maxim is an important tonic. The question of what tools we must have in the United States is important, but new tools alone are useless. To get through this trial, we will need the courage to use them.

A WAY FORWARD

Trump will at some point be gone, as is true for all of us. But other politicians will emulate him because Trump has proven the effectiveness of the brazen political lie. We must develop an antidote, one that is both wise and can withstand legal scrutiny under our own laws. Whatever solution we come up with must be compatible with our nation's values and laws, withstanding the sorts of challenges that brought down parts of the Stolen Valor Act.

To consider the options before us, let's examine three possible laws.

* * *

Imagine, first, that the US Congress has passed a new federal statute in the tradition of Brazil's "Clean Slate Law." Let's call this law the Truth in Elections Act (TEA) and codify it as Section 1001A, which would put it numerically right after the existing false-statement statute in Section 1001 of Title 18 of the United States Code (which is a repository of many of our nation's federal laws). The real-life Section 1001 law states:

> Whoever, in any matter within the jurisdiction of any department or agency of the United States knowingly and willfully falsifies, conceals, or covers up by any trick, scheme, or device a material fact, or makes any false, fictitious, or fraudulent statements or representations, or makes or uses any false writing or document knowing the same to contain any false, fictitious, or fraudulent statement or entry, shall be fined under this title or imprisoned not more than five years, or both.

This law has been interpreted broadly to cover lies to numerous federal officers. Here is an example from my twenty-plus years as a prosecutor: When I, along with an FBI agent, conducted witness interviews, I would advise the witnesses of their rights and obligations, including warning them that, even though not under oath, if they lied during the interview, they could be committing a crime under Section 1001 and face possible prosecution and jail. Pretty intimidating stuff, but that often was the point, in order to impress upon them the need to be truthful.

Our new hypothetical law, Section 1001A or TEA, extends the real-life Section 1001 — expanding its reach to lies that specifically target our electoral system:

> Anyone who knowingly and willfully makes any false, fictitious or fraudulent statement or representation about the election results or process in any federal election, with an intent to cast doubt on the integrity of the results or process, will have committed a civil offense for which disqualification from elected office may be imposed for up to 8 years. To be found liable for this offense, proof must be established beyond a reasonable doubt. A person found liable hereunder may take an immediate expedited appeal from the decision.

The TEA would apply to all federal elections, whether for the Senate, House, or White House. Yet because the law is civil in nature, it would not carry the possibility of jail for anyone found liable; they would simply be barred from holding office for a set period of time.

Now imagine that Congress has passed a second new law, another civil statute that mirrors the spirit of Brazil's "truth in advertising" requirement for that country's politicians. Our second hypothetical law requires that, in every federal election, a candidate must periodically publicly certify to the Federal Election Committee that all factual assertions they have made (or caused to be made on their behalf) during their campaign are truthful. The certification must provide the FEC with the factual basis for those assertions. If the candidate cannot so certify any statement they've made on the campaign trail, then that candidate must withdraw the statement in an FEC filing so that the public and press would have knowledge of that factual withdrawal prior to an election. Further, no candidate would be eligible for office without making the required filings; and presidential candidates would be ineligible for federal matching funds without filing these certifications and would have to return any such funds. Notably, as it is already a crime to knowingly and intentionally submit a false filing to a federal office, if the candidate's certifications contained an intentional and material falsehood, the candidate would be subject to criminal penalties for a false filing.

Finally, imagine a third new federal law that expands another existing US law, Section 2383 of Title 18. That law renders people ineligible to hold office if they have been convicted of the crimes of insurrection or rebellion. To that existing law, our new law adds the underlined language:

Whoever incites, sets on foot, assists, or engages in any rebellion or insurrection against the authority of the United States or the laws thereof, or gives aid or comfort thereto, <u>or knowingly and intentionally violates 18 U.S.C. section 1001A (the TEA)</u>, shall be fined under this title or imprisoned not more than ten years, or both; and shall be incapable of holding any office under the United States.

This new law adds criminal consequences, not simply debarment, for a violation of our hypothetical first law, the TEA.

Each of these three new laws would address, in different ways, the problem that our democracy faces from political lies; each presents different options for holding offenders accountable. Of course, although all three models are possible federal laws addressing federal elections, each of our fifty states could enact similar versions of all three statutes governing their respective state elections. In fact, many states already disqualify people from elected office if convicted of various crimes.

How might the three federal statutes fare under our constitutional regime? The surest way of course, to ensure these laws' constitutionality would be to amend the Constitution to explicitly permit these solutions. But I have avoided proposing that as a fix because of its practical improbability. It has been decades since the Constitution has been amended, and it is by wise design a difficult and tortuous course to chart. Sometimes too hard: even the proposed Equal Rights Amendment could not muster the necessary three-quarters of the states' votes for constitutional ratification. So it's only pragmatic to ask whether these statutory solutions could pass scrutiny under our existing Constitution.

The first two of these hypothetical laws would be the most resilient against constitutional challenge, with the third being the most vulnerable.

The first two hypothetical laws share an important feature of the Brazilian debarment law, which offers the most legally viable model for how we might deter political lies in the United States. The Brazilian law ensures the integrity of elections, but it does so without banning speech at all. Recall that Bolsonaro's election lies led to his disqualification from holding office, but the Brazilian debarment law did not prohibit his speech in the first place. In the same way, our first two hypothetical US laws — TEA and the FEC certification law — don't ban speech, either.

Rather, these laws circumscribe a person's right to run for public office — something for which, unlike the right to free speech, no right exists in either the United States or Brazil. Instead of prohibiting anyone's speech, the first two hypothetical US laws, like the Clean Slate Law in Brazil, simply pose a choice for anyone seeking to run for federal office: if you want to run for office, you cannot lie. Conversely, if you want to lie about the election, you're free to do so, but understandably the state has a valid interest in determining that you then cannot run for office.

Disqualifying someone from running in elections is, of course, a serious consequence both for that candidate and for anyone seeking to vote for them. But just as no person in Brazil, nor in the United States for that matter, has an absolute right to run for any office, neither does the electorate have the absolute right to have a particular person on the ballot. In fact, our Constitution places limits on qualifications necessary to run for president and, as we know from the Progressive movement in the early twentieth century, there are myriad statutory restrictions on who can be on a ballot. And numerous states already ban people convicted of various crimes from running for public office.

The first two of our hypothetical US laws have an added benefit, when compared to criminal debarment laws: because the two new laws are not criminal statutes, everyone subject to them can be called to explain themselves under oath. True, in both civil and criminal cases in the United States we enjoy a Fifth Amendment privilege to refuse to answer questions that would tend to incriminate us in a criminal matter. But in a civil case, unlike a criminal case, that refusal can be used against you by the judge or jury. What this means in the context of our hypothetical laws is that if a candidate refuses to explain the basis for a factual assertion, the court may presume that the assertion is untruthful or was not made in good faith. It is particularly fitting that candidates for public office who refuse to explain themselves have this presumption held against them.

Another particularly important benefit derives from the fact that the first two hypothetical laws are civil statutes: they would be impervious to presidential pardons. We have witnessed the president's pardon power eradicate righteous prosecutions of corrupt politicians, CEOs, insurrectionists, political allies, drug kingpins, and even murderers. The debarment remedy would be immune to this sort of abuse, because the pardon power applies only to criminal matters, not civil liability (and not to any state offenses, criminal or civil, at all). A president thus could not neuter the effect of the first two hypothetical laws.

For candidates for president, there is something particularly righteous about the second hypothetical law, less a constitutional strength per se than a condign justification for its existence. Candidates for the US presidency are eligible for federal matching funds. Federal taxpayers should rightly not be forced to pay to promote a candidate who is lying to their faces. The Federal Election Commission already has numerous filing requirements regarding candidates and sanctions for failing to file accurate reports;

the second of our hypothetical laws would add one more requirement, one that wouldn't restrict candidates' speech about their opinions or the policies they espouse. It would simply restrict their lies — false statements of fact.

Setting righteousness aside, the first of our two viable laws would be easier to defend, constitutionally, than the second — at least as I have written the two laws. That's because the first hypothetical law, TEA, does not attempt to regulate all political lies; rather, like the Brazilian law that it's modeled on, TEA is tailored to target only intentional lies about the election process, which are also the ones that could cause the most damage to a democracy. The second of our hypothetical US laws isn't limited to intentional lies about the election process, so it would be more vulnerable to the Supreme Court's scrutiny. It, of course, could be drafted to cover only false election lies, but for the sake of setting out the various legal frameworks at our disposal, I have started with the broader version of the model law.

This limited reach of the first hypothetical law could prove important if our imagined TEA ever finds itself before the Supreme Court. Recall the balancing approach reflected in all three of the opinions in the Supreme Court's *Alvarez* decision. If our hypothetical law goes before the Supreme Court, the Justices will weigh the governmental interest in passing the law against the scope of the law and harms it may impose on protected free speech. And the tighter tailoring of TEA is akin to the revised Stolen Valor Act of 2013 — the version after Congress narrowed the scope of that law to make it constitutional. With all due respect to the congressional desire not to cheapen the currency of military awards — the government's interest in the *Alvarez* case — it pales in comparison to our interest in maintaining faith in the election process and results. Without that faith, there can be no perceived valid elections. With no perceived valid elections, there can be no functioning democracy.

There is an important debate to be had about whether or not laws like the first two hypothetical laws I'm imagining here should be restricted to only lies about the electoral process or should cover other types of lies as well. Challengers to a broad law that covers all lies will contend that only the most pernicious lies should be subject to disqualification. They'll argue that a more nuanced approach is needed, one that reserves the penalty of debarment for the most potentially harmful lies. Some lies, these critics will argue, can be left for the electorate to judge and should not be subject to the draconian remedy of disqualification, such as lies about sex, one's decades-old academic record, one's wealth, the size of one's apartment in Trump Tower, or one's crowd size. They rightly can note that a broad legal prohibition would affect us all, not just the candidate, since it limits our electoral choices.

The more puritanical among us, on the other hand, will hold that any lie by a candidate should be subject to disqualification. Should we not expect the complete truth from people who have the privilege of representing the American public? Don't they owe "we, the people" a duty of loyalty? Have we become so inured to lies that we no longer expect the truth — leading to a cynical electorate that excuses political lies by saying, "They all do it"? It is high time that we put an end to this sorry state of affairs, these purists will say. We should be better — and we deserve better — than expecting our leaders to lie.

I admit that, in my heart of hearts, I'm one of the purists. We wouldn't tolerate for a second a lawyer lying to her client; that would be a violation of the attorney's fundamental legal duty of loyalty and candor to the people she represents. We should expect no less from candidates and politicians who are supposed to represent and serve us. (Forgive the analogy: I've been a lawyer for over forty years.) But while a purist at heart, I'm also a pragmatist. I want this problem to be fixed. And that means working inside of a constitutional system which argues for the most resilient and promising approach to our country's honesty crisis.

Whether we take a narrower or broader approach, either way we must draw some line between the lies we choose to punish and those we don't. The current approach is to draw no line at all. As a consequence, lies flourish that are deadly to the democratic process and that are swallowed whole by far too many Americans. Considering where to draw the line is important, but what is most important is that we do something—whether a broad or only narrow version of the second hypothetical law. I like to say to folks that the old adage, "If it ain't broke, don't fix it," also works in reverse. When it is broken, you must fix it.

There is one more proposed fix to our broken system, that found in the third hypothetical law. It is in many ways the most puritan, but for this reason would be the most challenging to implement in the United States. This is rightly so, because it is the most burdensome on free speech—even if it targets only intentionally false election lies. We can predict this with some confidence because of the Supreme Court's discussion in *Alvarez* about the chilling effect on protected speech when criminalizing even false speech. True, the Justices suggested only minor tweaks to the Stolen Valor Act to make it constitutional. But all three of the court's opinions were concerned that regulating false factual speech could have a chilling effect on truthful speech. In *Alvarez*, the majority of the Justices did not see how that concern would be of any real moment when dealing with a false claim to have received a military medal claim: How could prohibiting lies like that have the effect of chilling true speech? But we shouldn't expect the same conclusion when it comes to political speech — whether of the true or the false kind.

The Supreme Court could reasonably point out that our third hypothetical law, with its criminal penalties of fine and imprisonment for anyone who "knowingly and intentionally violates" TEA, could have a chilling effect on truthful speech as well as on lies. It's not hard to imagine candidates self-censoring edgy statements on the campaign trail — even if those statements arguably are true — in order to avoid risking the particularly dire consequences of our imagined criminal statute. And indeed, the Court surely would be particularly concerned about this chilling effect in the context of elections, which would make it all the more difficult for our hypothetical third law to pass the constitutional acid test.

Moreover, although our third hypothetical law adds one more crime (that of intentionally lying about an election) to two crimes that Congress already criminalizes and punishes with disqualification (that is, insurrection and rebellion), there is a gulf of difference between these crimes. The latter two do not resemble any activity remotely protected by the Constitution or pose the same risk of chilling protected First Amendment speech. The Constitution does not protect engaging in insurrection or rebellion — quite the contrary — so from a legal standpoint, those activities are fair game. The same cannot be said of making a false statement about an election, an activity that the Constitution also may not protect, but falls very close to activities that are protected by the Constitution (specifically, speech that's covered by the First Amendment).

All this is not to suggest that there is no possibility that the third hypothetical would pass constitutional muster. An argument in support of the third model's constitutionality is that it does not run afoul of the concerns raised by Justice Alito in *Alvarez*. For Alito, the problem with regulating certain false speech is that the state has no business getting into the business of deciding what is true and false speech, at least when it comes to banning speech concerning the areas of religion, history, philosophy, and the like. Alito rejected the idea that there is no objective truth; his concern was with the state telling us what we could and could not talk about — a position directly at odds with the German approach of banning Holocaust denial.

Our proposed third hypothetical does not raise this concern. The law leaves to a jury, not the government, to determine that a statement is intentionally false. Unlike the German Holocaust denial law, it is not banning speech on topics chosen by the government as *verboten*. It borrows instead a page from existing US defamation law, where civil juries decide every day precisely the same question. The same is true for the myriad criminal prosecutions for making false statements to the government that violate the existing law found in Section 1001. And the use of Section 1001 to prosecute a false FEC filing — required to be made by all candidates under the second model law — fits that description to a T. Neither a Section 1001 charge nor a charge under the third model are analogous to the German Holocaust law, which reflects a conclusive governmental pronouncement that speech on a certain subject is false. That runs afoul of Alito's reasoning. The same is not true of the proposed new laws, civil or criminal.

AN IMMUNITY DEFENSE

It's not hard to imagine a president or other government official running for office claiming that they're immune from prosecution for violating a law like the TEA. After all, Donald Trump famously grasped at this defense when he was accused of breaking real-life criminal federal laws, and the Supreme Court largely backed him up in articulating its new legal framework. So we need to be prepared for that same immunity argument to challenge implementation of a new hypothetical law, such as the TEA.

The good news is that the body of US law on presidential civil and criminal immunity — exemplified most recently by the Supreme Court's 2024 decision in the case memorably captioned *Trump v. United States* — should not provide a safe haven for candidates who lie, even those who may sit in our nation's most powerful office.

Recall that *Trump v. United States* arose from Trump's appeal in a federal criminal prosecution in Washington,

DC, for felonies that arose out of his efforts to remain in office after losing the 2020 election. Trump claimed that he had immunity from all the charges in that case. But neither the Supreme Court's resolution of this case, nor its immunity decisions in civil cases, provide candidates for political office a get-out-of-jail-free card for avoiding the strictures of a debarment law like the TEA.

Here is why candidates for office should not be able to claim immunity. In *Trump v. United States*, the Court broke down into three different categories the types of actions that a president might take. The first category covered official conduct by the president exercising authority that the Constitution gives to the president exclusively. The pardon power is one such power. Such powers belong only to the president, and Congress has no ability to limit that power through a federal statute. If, for example, Congress were to pass a law prohibiting presidents who have been involved in a crime from issuing pardons to conspirators, as sensible as we may think that law would be, the Supreme Court would strike it down as unconstitutional; it would usurp a power that the Constitution gives solely to the president. The only way to have that new law pass constitutional muster would be to amend the Constitution.

At the other extreme, in *Trump v. United States* the Court said there was a category of actions carried out by a president that are not taken in an official capacity. Those actions enjoy no immunity. That actions are taken even while a person is president does not mean that they are part of the president's official actions. The Court treats the actions in this category the same as actions taken before or after the person was president. No immunity would apply to actions the person took when running for office before their election, or as a sitting president while acting as a candidate seeking reelection. We have a real-life example as well: the charges against Trump in the New York State criminal case, in which he was convicted of filing false business records to conceal his scheme to win the 2016 election, would fall into this bucket.

The third category of presidential actions covers conduct that a president undertakes in an official capacity, but outside those areas that the Constitution gives to the president exclusively. There are a lot of these areas — zones in which Congress and the executive branch both have roles to play, such as health, education, and immigration policies. In these domains, the Supreme Court held in *Trump v. United States* that the president is entitled to at least presumptive immunity for his actions, immunity that can be rebutted only if the criminal action would "pose no 'dangers of intrusion'" on his presidential authority.

The Supreme Court did not decide the factual issue of what specific conduct alleged in the Trump indictment was not official conduct. Instead, it sent that question back to the trial court to decide in the first instance, but applying the legal framework it set out. At least four of the Justices made it clear, however, that they would not accord Trump immunity for the alleged conduct that he interfered with the state electoral processes. Justice Amy Coney Barrett wrote separately from the majority, to make clear that she viewed this conduct as not entitled to immunity, whereas the other five Justices in the majority simply did not reach that factual issue. Regardless of how they might have ruled on how its legal framework would apply to the specific factual allegations, the Court made clear that conduct not taken in an official capacity is not immunized, leaving open only the factual issue of whether the conduct was undertaken in that capacity.

How would the Court apply this tripartite framework to our hypothetical federal statute, Section 1001A? Of course, because the Supreme Court only handed down its presidential immunity decision in July 2024 and no additional court cases have built on it in the short time since, there is no decision directly addressing this question. That being said, there is a persuasive case to be made that the decision simply doesn't apply to our anti-lying law.

For one thing, the TEA, as you'll remember, is not a criminal statute; it's not even a typical civil statute subjecting a candidate to redress for damages or the other normal relief in a civil action. The criminal immunity decision in *Trump v. United States* simply does not apply to a civil law, let alone one that imposes only the remedy of disqualification. And even if it did, immunity does not apply to conduct undertaken as a candidate for office, even if the person is in office at the time and running for reelection.

But there's yet another reason to doubt the ability to use the *Trump v. United States* case to defeat the TEA: the vast majority of people running for federal office aren't the president of the United States. That decision was grounded in the unique nature of the presidency: if the new Section 1001A law were being applied to a candidate for a federal office who was not the current president seeking reelection, the presidential immunity decision would not afford that person immunity at all.

So far, we have looked at the question of whether the three hypothetical models could pass legal muster. But are any of the three particular hypothetical remedies worth the foreseeable costs? As doctors ask: Is the cure worse than the disease? This is akin to the two questions I always asked myself when I was a prosecutor: The first, and typically the easier, of the two questions to answer was whether I believed there was sufficient proof to indict and convict someone of a crime. The second, and often the harder, question was whether, once I had that requisite evidence, I should proceed. Should the particular person under investigation be charged with the crime that I had evidence they committed?

That's the question we turn to next.

THE LAW IN ACTION

Like any good lawyer — indeed, like any good citizen — I worry about laws being weaponized. I make no exception for the hypothetical law that I've suggested: Section 1001A of Title 18 of the United States Code, a law that could help us bring the problem of political lies under control in this country. Corrupt politicians and candidates will surely try to use a law like the TEA to disqualify political rivals. We have seen this movie before: Trump starred in it three times already.

The first Trump impeachment in 2019 was predicated on Trump engaging in this precise stratagem. The

House of Representatives impeachment was grounded on Trump's improperly withholding vital congressionally appropriated military aid to Ukraine, unless and until Ukraine announced that it was opening a criminal investigation into Trump's putative presidential rival, Joe Biden. Trump could then tout Biden's corruption to the American electorate without ever revealing that he had caused the announced investigation by putting a metaphorical gun to Ukraine's head.

That nefarious strategy was a new version of a scheme Trump had used in 2016, as set out by Manhattan prosecutors in their case against Trump, the only one of the four criminal cases against Trump to make it to trial. At that trial, the Manhattan district attorney presented evidence, notably including a firsthand account from the head of the *National Enquirer*, that Trump had made a secret deal with that media outlet to paint a rosy picture of his candidacy by killing negative stories, while also planting trumped-up stories against political adversaries—testimony that, surprisingly, went virtually unchallenged by the Trump defense team. The jury later went on to convict Trump on all thirty-four counts of falsifying business records.

We saw this gambit a third time, in the second impeachment proceeding of Donald Trump in January 2021, shortly before he left office after losing the presidential election to Biden. That impeachment centered on Trump's role in fomenting a plan to undermine the 2020 presidential election, culminating in the January 6 insurrection. A majority of both the House and Senate concluded that Trump had sought to obstruct the lawful counting of the electoral votes.

If this recent history is any guide, there can be no question that unscrupulous politicians will attempt to misuse any law that's expressly designed to disqualify people from running for office — which is exactly what our hypothetical law, the TEA, is meant to do.

But any legal tool can be misused, as the Trump administration reminds us daily. And no system of justice is perfect. No matter how high the standard of proof, judges and juries and appellate courts may get it wrong. We live with our legal system's institutional error rate in the most serious matters we confront as a society, including sending people to prison for life or even to their death.

There is no question that there is a risk of error or abuse in the case of a law like the TEA, but we have checks to prevent both within our legal system. In normal times, the Department of Justice itself is one such check. But even when that institution's norms are overcome by apparatchiks (as is evident in the Trump administration), there are other checks. Juries and judges need to be convinced of the claims. A high standard of proof, while not foolproof, mitigates the risk of abuse or error, which is why we have the highest standard under the law for determining criminal guilt: proof beyond a reasonable doubt (the standard that must be met in order to find liability in new Section 1001A to reduce the risk of error and abuse). And as we have seen time and again, a courtroom is one place where adjectives and epithets cannot stand in for actual proof. We do not need to speculate on the ability of courts to differentiate between the two: not a single court has vindicated the Trump lie of election fraud in the 2020 election.

Ultimately, how you weigh the risks and gravity of abuse depends, I think, not so much on your faith in trials as on your assessment of what is currently happening in America. If you do not think that the fate of our democracy is at stake today — if you think that we are in a pendulum swing that we will get through — then the idea of creating a tool that could be used to improperly disqualify legitimate opposition leaders may seem downright scary and not worth the potential benefits. You may reason that we don't want to have candidates for public office bogged down — or pushed out — by inappropriate efforts to disqualify them. You may think that if we simply are able to find a promising candidate, we can win the next election, even if it's in a squeaker. We can then breathe a sigh of relief. At least until the next election.

You may, on the other hand, be like me and view the situation we are in as an existential threat to the continuation of our democracy after 250 years. If you're of this view, then we have an imperative to strengthen our democratic tools, given the threats of authoritarianism backed by powerful financial and media sources.

This isn't to say that I don't fear abuse of a law like our hypothetical TEA. I worry that five Supreme Court Justices would use the new tool as a weapon to uphold the wrongful disqualification of a candidate who belongs to the opposing party of the president who nominated them. But if that occurs, our problem won't be this new law; it would be that we'd have lost our constitutional system of "checks and balances" that splits power among three branches of government, the better to preserve our liberty and rights. We would instead have an executive branch run amok, in a system that could better be described as "blank checks and no balance." Law would not be a salvation; it would be powerless to protect us.

Assuming that it's used in the way it's intended, how would an anti-lying law like the one we've conceived work in practice? There are far too many politicians, candidates, and lies to discuss all the possible permutations, but there are some useful scenarios that show us how the law could function to both deter and punish political liars.

The new debarment law could apply to any candidate for Congress or the presidency or vice presidency, the offices of our federal government to which people must be elected rather than appointed to their positions; for instance, if it had been law at the time, it could have been used against Donald Trump after he lost the 2020 election and repeatedly touted, among other falsehoods, the 2020 election fraud lie.

In reality, however, the law would likely be used less against people running for the Senate or the presidency than against candidates for the House, because the former terms of office are longer (six and four years, respectively) and there are fewer of these offices than there are in the House of Representatives (101 versus 435). So the new debarment law would most commonly apply to a candidate running for the House of Representatives, a two-year federal position.

Imagine that one such candidate, an aspiring member of the US House of Representatives, intentionally lies about the results of the 2020 election. In order to avoid getting slapped with a civil lawsuit, as Rudy Giuliani and Fox were, the candidate doesn't make the mistake of alleging that any specific person or company participated in the 2020 election fraud; rather, she simply alleges that the election was infected by fraud, and that Donald Trump actually won. (Or, if you like, imagine that someone on the other side of the political aisle tells a similar lie, intentionally claiming that Kamala Harris actually won the 2024 presidential election.)

This hypothetical candidate loses the election for Congress and the government sues her under the new Section

1001A law. After a full trial at which she testifies, a civil jury finds that her statement was intentionally false, citing proof beyond a reasonable doubt — say, that the candidate had no evidence of fraud, that courts had repeatedly found no fraud, and that she had privately been told there was no such fraud. The judge upholds the jury finding and bars her from holding federal office for five years. The candidate appeals these findings, but her appeal is denied.

In this scenario, the law has served its purpose. It removes a political liar from the pool of candidates for federal office; it also deters other people from following in her footsteps. Bolsonaro is a good example of this dual goal in action.

Lest we are inundated with bogus claims that candidates have lied, the courts could create barriers to such claims. The courts have tackled this same problem in many areas of the law in order to thwart opening the floodgates to harassing lawsuits. In the securities law which regulates the stock market, the courts have created various hurdles to prevent the avaricious from bringing a civil case merely because the price of a company's stock drops. The same is true in defamation cases. The courts require more than that bare-bones allegation to sustain a civil case. Instead, plaintiffs seeking to bring civil lawsuits must enumerate specific factual allegations to support their claims. Without those specific factual allegations, the case is dismissed outright. So, too, the court could require a claim of intentional falsity to allege specific facts that would support the claim that the statement is both factually wrong and that the speaker knew it was false at the time.

There is an important permutation on how the law would work. Our hypothetical TEA, which focuses solely on the remedy of debarment from holding office for lying about the election, is only going to deter a would-be liar who wants to hold public office, whether they're a first-time candidate or running for reelection. The law wouldn't be of use against a person who has absolutely no interest in holding public office in the future. For a liar like that, the threat posed by Section 1001A would be about as effective as a threat to cancel a Baptist family's Passover seder.

Similarly, a debarment statute like the TEA would rarely deter lies from a president who cannot seek reelection because he has served two terms, which is the maximum permitted by the Constitution, no matter what Trump might like the law to be. One exception would be the rare president who thereafter seeks to hold another elected office; that has occurred precisely twice, when Presidents John Quincy Adams and Andrew Johnson served in Congress after being president. But normally, the penalty of debarment would be of little consequence to a president who has already been elected twice.

There is one other unusual scenario where even a two-term president might worry about a debarment law. At the time of this writing, there has been talk about how

Trump might finagle his way functionally into a "third term." If Trump ran for *vice* president, a debarment law could prevent his holding that office if he violated the TEA. That would be true whether or not he was seeking that office in order to remain in the number-two position (and find a factotum to serve as "president"), or if the new president resigned so that Vice President Trump could then claim to be president. In either case, the threat of debarment remedy really could deter Trump from spreading the worst sort of political lies, lest he be barred from public office as Bolsonaro or Marine le Pen have been in Brazil and France, respectively.

Even if a two-term president were not deterred by this new law, the debarment law would still have significant teeth. It would apply to a president's political acolytes who repeat his election lies. If, for instance, the price for being part of the second Trump administration is lying about fraud in the 2020 election, the debarment law would subject an ambitious toady to disqualification. If, hypothetically, JD Vance or Marco Rubio violated Section 1001A, they could be barred from holding future public office, just as Bolsonaro was in Brazil or as people convicted of crimes are in numerous US states.

In short, current politicians would have to think twice about whether they want to jeopardize their future career prospects. Should they lie to stay in the current good graces of the president and risk debarment, or instead take the less risky path of keeping mum and preserving the ability to seek higher office? Any resulting lack of support from those acolytes refusing to promulgate the presidential lie would be salutary. It would mitigate the virulence of the election lie.

Another permutation on how a debarment law would operate in practice concerns removing a public official currently in office. The person could be barred from holding elected office in the future, but the Constitution limits the ability to remove an elected official from their current office. Removing a president or a member of Congress from office is governed by the Constitution. A model debarment statute can work to preclude someone from attaining office (whether as a new candidate or seeking reelection), but removal cannot be governed by a statute because of the basic tenet in the law that a statute cannot override the Constitution. We are all aware from the two Trump impeachment proceedings of the hurdles the Constitution places on removal, but that is the process we have, unless the Constitution is amended.

This is where the second and third model laws can play a role, as they both can lead to criminal sanctions, including on people currently in elected office. Just like anyone running for office, current politicians can face prosecution if they lie, as Enron's Kenneth Lay and Jeffrey Skilling did with their false representations about that company. The Sword of Damocles these new hypothetical criminal statutes create could operate to deter the lie in the first place, as well as punish the brazen politician who nevertheless chooses to lie.

The elephant in the room, of course, is the president's ability to effectively nullify the hypothetical criminal statutes through his use of the pardon power. A sitting president has the power under the Constitution to pardon a person for any and all federal crimes (but not violations of civil statutes). No future president can undo that pardon. Any member of Congress could therefore weigh the likelihood of such a pardon against the chance of being prosecuted and convicted for a crime. The president may be able to even pardon himself for a criminal offense, but that issue has not (yet) been decided by the Supreme Court. The argument against being able to "self-pardon" is that the Constitution did not suppose the president could be both judge and jury in his own case. The argument for the power to self-pardon is that the language of the pardon power in the Constitution is broad and provides no obvious exception. We fortunately have not had to confront that issue, but we may going forward.

Where does all this leave us? We have seen the tools that have been developed in other democracies to deal with a problem that is common to our country as well. And those tools have worked, without so far running the risk of wrongful debarment or prosecution. These tools can be adapted to our democracy, while respecting our

Constitution. They can be part of our effort to rebuild an edifice that is teetering under the weight of deceit, before it is too late.

In sum, the threat to democracy is real. The tools to deal with the threat exist. The time to implement them is now, while truth still matters. Our democracy depends on it.

CONCLUSION

This book is meant to be a sobering dissection of an urgent problem facing our country: our body politic is vulnerable to political lies, and our laws have so far failed to protect this Achilles heel. We need to adapt, lest the next dissection be part of an autopsy.

The book is also meant to be galvanizing. Legal norms, once broken, rarely fully self-repair. That is why I've addressed targeted proposals: laws that disqualify from public office, for a set term, those who knowingly and intentionally lie about the conduct or outcome of an election. They do not prohibit speech. They impose consequences for false factual statements — through a fair process and high evidentiary burden — by those who seek to gain power through deceiving the electorate about the most foundational mechanism of our democracy.

The legal tools that I'm proposing are not unprecedented. When confronted with similar threats, other democracies have taken action — some by imposing even more stringent sanctions than the ones I've suggested. Germany, after the unimaginable crimes of World War II, enacted a law against Holocaust denial. France barred a leading political candidate from holding office for five years after she was convicted of fraud. Brazil barred Jair Bolsonaro from office for eight years for knowingly spreading lies about its electoral system; its laws also call for people who spread misinformation about elections to be jailed, but Bolsonaro ended up in prison for another reason — plotting a coup to hold onto power after losing the country's 2022 presidential election.

Brazil and France withhold the sacred privilege of representing the public from anyone who has been found to have broken core societal bonds. All three countries use the law to preserve personal or democratic integrity. So, too, do most states in our union, barring candidates from office if they have been convicted of a crime.

Our nation's founding document should not prevent these reforms. Supreme Court Justice Robert Jackson reminded us that the Constitution is not "a suicide pact." It does not require us to stand by while our institutions are systematically hollowed out by deliberate, unchecked deception. If we do, what we will have left is the veneer of a democracy, no more substantial than a plywood stage in a John Ford Western.

Our system of government, built on checks and balances, has faltered in the face of a political culture increasingly indifferent to truth, and with no functioning forum to separate fiction from fact. Combine this with a balkanization of news, the rise of Silicon Valley robber barons wielding algorithms that skew our impressions of reality, and the hegemony of executive power over the other branches of government, and you have a toxic stew.

But it doesn't have to be this way. Just as we can learn from countries around the world who have tried and succeeded in tackling problems like the ones we face today, we can also take inspiration from Americans who have seen these threats coming, and who have urged us to take action. We can learn from Justice Robert Jackson who, in his famous 1952 concurrence in the *Youngstown Steel* case, warned of the "grave dangers" that the exorbitant power of the presidency poses for a democracy. The *Youngstown* decision disallowed President Truman from unilaterally taking over steel mills, which were set to temporarily close during a strike, in order to continue furnishing steel for the country's war effort in Korea.

In his concurring opinion, Jackson was not speaking in the abstract about the problem of unchecked executive power. He had seen firsthand the risk of authoritarianism. In 1945, President Truman had selected Jackson — who was then a sitting Supreme Court Justice — to be the chief

American prosecutor at the first Nuremberg trial. Jackson took a leave from the Court, and along with his fellow prosecutors from Europe and Russia, presented the prosecution's evidence against the first of the Nazi defendants to be tried there.

After his return to the Supreme Court, Jackson warned in *Youngstown* of the current risk posed by unchecked executive power. Jackson pointedly noted, with a force that his personal biography imbued in his words, that the German president after World War I, and without the concurrence of its legislative body in the Reichstag, was empowered to temporarily suspend individual rights in the name of public safety. "This proved a temptation to every government," Jackson wrote, culminating with Hitler's suspending all such rights, never to be restored.

Jackson warned that "emergency powers...tend to kindle emergencies." The death and destruction that Hitler wrought across the globe was stopped only by a global war. And the millions and millions of victims of his crimes were left to be commemorated on the Île de la Cité in Paris, the beaches of Normandy, and in countless other memorials and graves.

Justice Jackson, turning to the lessons for Americans, warned of the risk from the dramatic growth of power of the United States presidency since the founding of the nation in the late eighteenth century. This centralization of power was, he observed, unforeseen by the framers of our

Constitution, noting the gap between the president's power on "paper" in the Constitution and the actual, practical powers of the office:

> In drama, magnitude, and finality his decisions so far overshadow any others that almost alone he fills the public mind through modern methods of communications. By his prestige as head of state and his influence upon public opinion he exerts a leverage upon those who are supposed to check and balance his power which often cancels their effectiveness.

Jackson made his observation in the mid-twentieth century; his words are truer today, and are all the more salient in our age where propaganda is left unchecked in the balkanized media and lies are permitted to serve as instruments of political dominance.

How shall we respond today to unchecked executive power, fueled by lies? To take a stand, we do not have to believe that absolutist power and egregious falsehoods will lead to the unthinkable consequences that Justice Jackson saw firsthand. We can deplore Trump's praising of Nazi sympathizers in Charlottesville as "fine people" without taking literally the warning from JD Vance (since reneged on after being promoted to Trump's VP running mate in 2024) that Trump is "America's Hitler." But we cannot ignore the risks either. The demise of democracy in a web of lies is surely not ameliorated by it paling in comparison to Nazi Germany.

What should be our collective response now? So far, it has been hope. Hope that institutions will hold. Hope that voters will see through the fog. Hope that facts will reclaim their footing.

Of course, the proposals I put forth, drawing on these international examples, can be criticized as insufficient. Are they the proverbial lipstick on a pig? A Band-Aid that does not address more fundamental problems?

In my mind's eye, I return to the conversation with my father and mother at that Saturday lunch in New York, where we discussed Joseph McCarthy and Donald Trump. In a conversation I can no longer actually have, I can hear my mother, ever the psychologist, asking me how this book contends with the deeper question of why these problems are arising in the first place. If you don't identify the root cause of an issue, how can you hope to ultimately fix it? This is a question a Freudian psychologist, or a political scientist for that matter, would certainly ponder.

I would answer my mom thus: Your observation is entirely valid, but it unfairly underrates the work performed in the moment by a Band-Aid. It serves to staunch bleeding and keeps a wound from infection. The remedy proposed here is surely not all we need to do; there are countless other proposals. This book is one such proposal and certainly not the answer to all our ills. But falling back on the bromide that we need to have more and better education and teach civics is, while undoubtedly true, hardly an effective response. That is a possible long-term solution for a democracy in need of salvation now. When you hit an iceberg, the captain's first instinct should not be to call for investment in better radar.

History teaches us where apathy and appeasement can lead. American democracy has survived many trials, but its survival is no more guaranteed than the permanence of buildings like Notre-Dame de Paris. Rather, endurance is the product of courageous choices — by lawmakers, by courts, by citizens. As Abraham Lincoln observed with respect to a nineteenth-century American crisis, the tactics of General Grant, not General McClellan, are required.

Today, we face a choice of our own. Do we allow the deliberate erosion of truth in the name of a nonexistent "right to lie"? Or do we act to preserve a shared factual foundation for democratic decision-making? When lies about election integrity go unchecked and become party orthodoxy, we are no longer voting in a democracy. We are voting in a hall of distorting funhouse mirrors, wherein many of us believe that we are seeing the world as it is.

Yes, any legal tool can be misused. That is why the rule of law demands procedures that are robust, neutral, and transparent. But the mere possibility of misuse is not a reason for inaction. It is a reason for care. The greater danger lies in doing nothing.

Like the rebuilders of Notre-Dame, we are called not merely to restore, but to fortify. Justice Jackson, having seen the fragility of law in the face of unchecked power, left us with this final reminder in *Youngstown*. The institutions of our democracy "may be destined to pass away." But it was "the duty of the Court to be last, not first, to give them up." That too is our duty as citizens.

ACKNOWLEDGMENTS

Jack Smith, at an interview I conducted with him at the Global Centre for Constitutional Democracy at University College London Faculty of Laws in the fall of 2025, noted that President Trump's attacks on him have had the effect of revealing who his true friends are. That struck a chord with me. This book would not have been possible without the support of many fearless friends and colleagues, as well as intrepid literary agents, lawyers, academic institutions in the United States and abroad, one publishing house, and a particularly skilled, dogged, and patient editor. They all know who they are. They have meant the world to me and have my unyielding gratitude and respect.

NOTES

Epigraph

vii. Hannah Arendt, "Truth and Politics," in *Between Past and Future* (New York: Viking, 1961), 252.

Introduction

2. *the Russia hoax*: Hope Yen et al., "AP fact check: Trump's exaggerations about the Russia probe," *PBS News*, April 1, 2019, https://www.pbs.org/newshour/politics/ap-fact-check-trumps-exaggerations-about-the-russia-probe.

2. *the 1950s Red Scare*: Landon R. Y. Storrs, "McCarthyism and the Second Red Scare," *Oxford Research Encyclopedia of American History*, July 2, 2015, 6–8.

3. *Germans marched into Austria*: William Carr, *Arms, Autarky, and Aggression: A Study in German Foreign Policy, 1933–1939* (London: Edward Arnold, 1972), 81–86.

4. *America's Hitler*: Gram Slattery and Helen Coster, "JD Vance once compared Trump to Hitler. Now, he is Trump's vice president-elect," Reuters, November 6, 2024, https://www.reuters.com/world/us/jd-vance-once-compared-trump-hitler-now-they-are-running-mates-2024-07-15/.

5. *German Nazi Party*: "Architecture at the service of memory: the memorial to the martyrs of the Deportation," France Ministry of Culture, accessed October 8, 2025, https://journeesdupatrimoine.culture.gouv.fr/w/377623/evenement/18811771/larchitecture-au-service-de-la-memoire-le-memorial-des-martyrs-de-la-deportation#/events/18811771.

6. *power goes unchecked*: "A Different Kind of Training: What New Agents Learn from the Holocaust," Federal Bureau of Investigation, March 30, 2010, https://archives.fbi.gov/archives/news/stories/2010/march/leas_033010/a-different-kind-of-training-what-new-agents-learn-from-the-holocaust.

6. *supporting its metal roof*: Aurelien Breeden et al., "Notre-Dame Attic Was Known as 'the Forest.' And It Burned Like One.," *New York Times*, April 16, 2019,

https://www.nytimes.com/2019/04/16/world/europe/why-notre-dame-fire
-spread.html.

7. *primary construction materials*: Michael Kimmelman, "A Miracle: Notre-Dame's
Astonishing Rebirth from the Ashes," *New York Times*, December 5, 2024,
https://www.nytimes.com/interactive/2024/12/05/arts/design/notre-dame
-reopens-paris.html.

8. *perceived Trump enemies*: "Rescinding Security Clearances and Access to
Classified Information from Specified Individuals," The White House, March
22, 2025, https://www.whitehouse.gov/presidential-actions/2025/03/rescinding
-security-clearances-and-access-to-classified-information-from-specified
-individuals/.

9. *my last name*: Tulsi Gabbard (@DNIGabbard), "Per @POTUS directive, I have
revoked security clearances and barred access to classified information for
Antony Blinken, Jake Sullivan, Lisa Monaco, Mark Zaid, Norman Eisen, Letitia
James, Alvin Bragg, and Andrew Weissman," X, March 10, 2025, https://x.com
/DNIGabbard/status/1899176257406857274.

9. *critical American interests*: "Addressing Risks from Jenner & Block," The White
House, March 25, 2025, https://www.whitehouse.gov/presidential-actions/2025
/03/addressing-risks-from-jenner-block/.

9. *transgender clients*: *Susman Godfrey LLP v. Exec. Off. of President*, No. 25-1107,
2025 WL 1779830 (D.D.C. June 27, 2025); "Preventing Abuses of the Legal
System and the Federal Court," The White House, March 22, 2025, https:
//www.whitehouse.gov/presidential-actions/2025/03/preventing-abuses-of-the
-legal-system-and-the-federal-court/.

9. *Mueller investigation*: The White House, "Jenner & Block."

10. *values and priorities*: Ibid.

10. *describe me*: WSJ News, "Trump Expands Retribution Against Law Firms in
New Executive Order," March 25, 2025, *YouTube*, 0:52, https://www.youtube
.com/watch?v=U4qwt63hDag; Nicholas Riccardi, "'Scum,' 'crooked' elections,
and 'corrupt' media. What Trump said inside the Justice Department," *AP
News*, March 15, 2025, https://apnews.com/article/trump-bondi-patel-justice
-fbi-retribution-ec275e730c6e75f2d6ee29eeec30fa07. Trump has continued in
that vein, from the Oval Office. See: Glenn Thrush, "Trump Names More Foes
He Wants Prosecuted as Bondi and Patel Look On," *New York Times*, October
15, 2025, https://www.nytimes.com/2025/10/15/us/politics/trump-bondi-patel
-blanche-oval-office.html.

10. *enemies of that state*: Lee Moran, "Stephen Miller Throws On-Air Tantrum
After MSNBC Analyst Dares To Question Trump," *HuffPost*, March 18, 2025,
https://www.huffpost.com/entry/stephen-miller-andrew-weissmann_n
_67d91081e4b011fc2140fa24.

10. *drew presidential disdain*: *Jenner & Block LLP v. U.S. Dep't of Just.*, 784 F. Supp. 3d
76, 94 (D.D.C. 2025). Trump would later call for me to be investigated; he did so
the day after the release of a video of a public interview I conducted with former
Special Counsel Jack Smith at the Global Centre for Constitutional Democracy
in London. Jack Smith, "The State of the United States: A Conversation with
Jack Smith," moderated by Andrew Weissmann, October 14, 2025, University

College London Faculty of Laws, *YouTube*, 1:16:41, https://www.youtube.com /watch?v=DR79GW6SvxE; Thrush, "Trump Names More Foes."

11. *government and public officials*: Ibid.

11. *null and void*: Ibid., 118. The Trump administration is appealing this and the other three unanimous judicial decisions striking down the executive orders targeting law firms.

11. *cowed into submission*: Michael S. Schmidt et al., "Law Firms Made Deals With Trump. Now He Wants More From Them.," *New York Times*, April 16, 2025, https://www.nytimes.com/2025/04/16/us/politics/law-firms-deals-trump.html.

11. *Trump and his allies*: Cerys Davies, "YouTube, Disney, and Meta have all settled. Inside President Trump's $90-million payday," *Los Angeles Times*, October 1, 2025, https://www.latimes.com/entertainment-arts/business/story/2025-10-01 /youtube-latest-company-to-settle-with-trump-disney-paramount-meta- 90-million.

11. *critical scientific grants*: Cecelia Smith-Schoenwalder, "Tracking Trump's Crack-down on Higher Education," *U.S. News & World Report*, October 3, 2025, https:// www.usnews.com/news/national-news/articles/trumps-higher-education -crackdown-visa-revocations-dei-bans-lawsuits-and-funding-cuts.

12. *influential segments of Europe*: Karl Popper, *The Open Society and Its Enemies* (London: Routledge, 1945).

13. *fact from fiction*: *Abrams v. United States*, 250 U.S. 616, 630 (1919) (Holmes, J., dissenting).

13. *deciding factual issues*: Ari Ezra Waldman, "The Marketplace of Fake News," *University of Pennsylvania Journal of Constitutional Law* 20 (2018): 869 ("The marketplace of ideas was always meant to be a marketplace of ideas, not *facts*.").

15. *devise reforms*: Ione Wells and Vanessa Buschschlüter, "Bolsonaro sentenced to 27 years in prison for plotting Brazil coup," *BBC*, September 11, 2025, https:// www.bbc.com/news/articles/c8xrqxk9p4xo.

Chapter 1

17. *with abandon and impunity*: Merlyn Thomas and Mike Wendling, "Trump repeats baseless claim about Haitian immigrants eating pets," *BBC*, September 15, 2024, https://www.bbc.com/news/articles/c77l28myezko; Sophie Tatum and Jim Acosta, "Report: Trump continues to question Obama's birth certificate," *CNN*, November 29, 2017, https://www.cnn.com/2017/11/28/politics/donald -trump-barack-obama-birth-certificate-nyt.

17. *average of 20.9 each day*: Glenn Kessler, "Trump made 30,573 false or misleading claims as president. Nearly half came in his final year.," *Washington Post*, January 23, 2021, https://www.washingtonpost.com/politics/how-fact -checker-tracked-trump-claims/2021/01/23/ad04b69a-5c1d-11eb-a976-bad6431e03e2 _story.html. The *New York Times* also kept track of Trump's lies during his first year in office. See: David Leonhardt and Stuart A. Thompson, "Trump's Lies," *New York Times*, December 14, 2017, https://www.nytimes.com/interactive/2017 /06/23/opinion/trumps-lies.html.

18. *scorecard was discontinued*: David Folkenflik, "Bezos' changes at 'Washing-ton Post' lead to mass subscription cancellations—again," *NPR*, February 26,

2025, https://www.npr.org/2025/02/28/nx-s1-5312819/washington-post-bezos-subscriptions-cancellations; Melvin Goodman, "Washington Post: Losing Credibility and Reporters," *CounterPunch*, September 29, 2025, https://www.counterpunch.org/2025/09/29/washington-post-losing-credibility-and-reporters/.

18. *Republicans hold that belief*: Rachel Weiner et al., "Republican loyalty to Trump, rioters climbs in 3 years after Jan. 6 attack," *Washington Post*, January 2, 2024, https://www.washingtonpost.com/dc-md-va/2024/01/02/jan-6-poll-post-trump/.

18. *but then did not do so*: Vaughn Hillyard and Garrett Haake, "Trump scraps plans to release 'irrefutable report' claiming election fraud in Georgia," *NBC News*, August 17, 2023, https://www.nbcnews.com/politics/donald-trump/trump-scraps-plans-releasing-report-georgia-election-rcna100515.

18. *advised him not to do so*: Ibid.

18. *return government documents to the government*: Alan Feuer, "Trump Was Warned to Return Records to Archives, Unsealed Documents Say," *New York Times*, April 22, 2024, https://www.nytimes.com/2024/04/22/us/politics/trump-warning-classified-documents-case.html.

18. *such evidence public*: Hillyard and Haake, "Trump Scraps Plan"; "Results of Lawsuits Regarding the 2020 Elections," Campaign Legal Center, https://campaignlegal.org/results-lawsuits-regarding-2020-elections.

19. *Fortune no. 7 public company*: Kristen Hays and Anna Driver, "Former Enron CEO Skilling's sentence cut to 14 years," Reuters, June 21, 2013, https://www.reuters.com/article/business/former-enron-ceo-skillings-sentence-cut-to-14-years-idUSBRE95K125/.

19. *that is, with a "b"*: Dan Ackman, "Enron The Incredible," *Forbes*, January 15, 2002, https://www.forbes.com/2002/01/15/0115enron.html.

19. *filed for bankruptcy*: "Enron files for bankruptcy," *BBC*, December 3, 2001, http://news.bbc.co.uk/2/hi/business/1688550.stm.

19. *corporate fraud in American history*: Simon Constable, "How the Enron Scandal Changed American Business Forever," *Time*, December 2, 2021, https://time.com/6125253/enron-scandal-changed-american-business-forever/.

20. *a large multicolor "E"*: *The Crooked E: The Unshredded Truth about Enron*, film directed by Penelope Spheeris, Culver City, CA: Robert Greenwald Productions, 2003.

20. *charging Lay with fraud*: David Streitfeld and Dana Calvo, "Jury Indicts Lay, Former Head of Enron," *Los Angeles Times*, July 8, 2004, https://www.latimes.com/archives/la-xpm-2004-jul-08-fi-enron8-story.html. I was the head of the Enron Task Force when Lay was indicted; it was tried by other team members when it later went to trial.

21. *his deceptive conduct*: "Enron Verdict: Ken Lay Guilty on All Counts, Skilling on 19 Counts," *ABC News*, May 25, 2006, https://abcnews.go.com/Business/LegalCenter/story?id=2003728&page=1.

21. *before he was to be sentenced*: Jeremy W. Peters and Simon Romero, "Enron Founder Dies Before Sentencing," *New York Times*, July 5, 2006, https://www.nytimes.com/2006/07/05/business/05cnd-lay.html.

21.   *verdicts for error*: Kate Murphy, "Judge Throws Out Kenneth Lay's Conviction," *New York Times*, October 18, 2006, https://www.nytimes.com/2006/10/18/business/judge-throws-out-kenneth-lays-conviction.html.

21.   *died of a massive heart attack*: Chad Abraham, "Coroner Confirms Lay Had Blocked Arteries," *Aspen Times*, July 19, 2006, https://www.aspentimes.com/news/coroner-confirms-lay-had-blocked-arteries/.

·21.   *he abruptly stepped down*: ABC News, "Enron Verdict."

21.   *when he suddenly resigned*: Richard A. Oppel Jr. and Alex Berenson, "Enron's Chief Executive Quits After Only 6 Months in Job," *New York Times*, August 15, 2001,   https://www.nytimes.com/2001/08/15/business/enron-s-chief-executive-quits-after-only-6-months-in-job.html.

21.   *even back in 2001*: ABC News, "Enron Verdict."

21.   *subpoenaed to testify*: "Skilling Lied About Stock Sale, U.S. Says," *Los Angeles Times*, January 5, 2006, https://www.latimes.com/archives/la-xpm-2006-jan-05-fi-skilling5-story.html.

22.   *attacks on the United States*: Ibid.; *United States v. Skilling*, 554 F.3d 529, 592–93 (5th Cir. 2009).

22.   *dramatically as a result*: *United States v. Skilling*, 554 F.3d at 592–93.

22.   *Skilling placed an order*: Ibid.

22.   *order to prove it*: "Skilling Lied," *Los Angeles Times*.

22.   *jury that convicted Lay*: *United States v. Skilling*, 554 F.3d at 542; *ABC News*, "Enron Verdict."

22.   *under the securities laws*: Ellen E. Schultz, "Enron Employees to Settle Retirement Lawsuit For $85 Million," *Wall Street Journal*, June 18, 2008, https://archive.is/EQy0K.

23.   *from losing precious savings*: Ibid.

23.   *on the regulatory tests*: "Volkswagen to Spend Up to $14.7 Billion to Settle Allegations of Cheating Emissions Tests and Deceiving Customers on 2.0 Liter Diesel Vehicles," *United States Department of Justice*, June 28, 2016, https://www.justice.gov/archives/opa/pr/volkswagen-spend-147-billion-settle-allegations-cheating-emissions-tests-and-deceiving.

24.   *pretended to be incompetent*: Selwyn Raab, "Vincent Gigante, Mafia Leader Who Feigned Insanity, Dies at 77," *New York Times*, December 19, 2005, https://www.nytimes.com/2005/12/19/obituaries/vincent-gigante-mafia-leader-who-feigned-insanity-dies-at-77.html.

24.   *days of stubble*: Ibid.

24.   *the Oddfather*: Ibid.

24.   *absent from the charges*: Arnold H. Lubasch, "U.S. Jury Convicts Eight as Members of Mob Commission," *New York Times*, November 20, 1986, https://www.nytimes.com/1986/11/20/nyregion/us-jury-convicts-eight-as-members-of-mob-commission.html.

24.   *the indictment was coming down*: *United States v. Gigante*, 925 F. Supp. 967, 973 (E.D.N.Y. 1996).

24.   *Gigante had by then ruled*: Raab, "Vincent Gigante."

24.   *girlfriend in New York*: Ibid.

24.   *were named Olympia*: Ibid.

24.   *Upper East Side town house*: Ibid.

24. *back of the town house*: Joseph P. Fried, "An F.B.I. Agent Testifies About Spying on Gigante," *New York Times*, June 27, 1997, https://www.nytimes.com/1997/06/27 /nyregion/an-fbi-agent-testifies-about-spying-on-gigante.html.

25. *incapable of such activities*: Ibid.

25. *inside the town house*: Ibid.

25. *Charlie then described the inside*: Ibid.

26. *competent to stand trial*: *United States v. Gigante*, 925 F. Supp. at 977.

26. *counts by a jury*: *United States v. Gigante*, 982 F. Supp. 140, 153 (E.D.N.Y. 1997); Blaine Harden, "Gigante Guilty of Racketeering, Conspiracy," *Washington Post*, July 25, 1997, https://www.washingtonpost.com/archive/politics/1997/07/26/gigante -guilty-of-racketeering-conspiracy/529f7ba5-6008-4c72-9351-d0226f65b930/.

26. *illness to avoid prosecution*: Andy Newman, "Gigante Says He Was Crazy…Like a Fox," *New York Times*, April 8, 2003, https://www.nytimes.com/2003/04/08 /nyregion/gigante-says-he-was-crazy-like-a-fox.html.

27. *won it by a landslide*: Brian Naylor, "Read Trump's Jan. 6 Speech, A Key Part Of Impeachment Trial," *NPR*, February 10, 2021, https://www.npr .org/2021/02/10/966396848/read-trumps-jan-6-speech-a-key-part-of -impeachment-trial.

27. *similar public statements*: Christina Wilkie, "Politics Trump Tries to Claim Victory Even as Ballots are Being Counted in Several States — NBC Has Not Made a Call," *CNBC*, November 4, 2020, https://www.cnbc.com/2020/11/04 /trump-tries-to-claim-victory-even-as-ballots-are-being-counted-in -several-states-nbc-has-not-made-a-call.html.

27. *millions of people who voted illegally*: Donald J. Trump (@realDonaldTrump), "In addition to winning the Electoral College in a landslide, I won the popular vote if you deduct the millions of people who voted illegally," X, November 27, 2016, https://x.com/realDonaldTrump/status/802972944532209664; Susan B. Glasser, "The President Is Acting Crazy, So Why Are We Shrugging It Off?," *New Yorker*, December 3, 2020, https://www.newyorker.com/news/letter-from -trumps-washington/the-president-is-acting-crazy-so-why-are-we-shrugging -it-off.

27. *No way*: Donald J. Trump (@realDonaldTrump), "Just saw the vote tabulations. There is NO WAY Biden got 80,000,000 votes!!! This was a 100% RIGGED ELECTION," X, November 26, 2020, https://x.com/realDonaldTrump/status /1331987171700510720; Donald J. Trump (@realDonaldTrump), "NO WAY WE LOST THIS ELECTION!," X, November 29, 2020, https://x.com /realDonaldTrump/status/1333245684011642881.

27. *history of our country*: John L. Dorman, "Trump, without evidence, calls the 2020 presidential election results 'the greatest fraud in the history of our country from an electoral standpoint,'" *Business Insider*, November 29, 2020, https://www.businessinsider.com/trump-fox-interview-bartiromo-debunked -fraud-allegations-election-2020-11.

27. *Tremendous evidence*: Donald J. Trump (@realDonaldTrump), "Tremendous evidence pouring in on voter fraud. There has never been anything like this in our Country!," X, December 15, 2020, https://x.com/realDonaldTrump /status/1338871862315667456.

NOTES

27. *conspiracy theory*: Donald J. Trump (@realDonaldTrump), "VOTER FRAUD IS NOT A CONSPIRACY THEORY, IT IS A FACT!!!," X, December 24, 2020, https://x.com/realDonaldTrump/status/1342212651447967744.

28. *The 2020 election*: Donald J. Trump (@realDonaldTrump), Truth Social, June 20, 2025, https://truthsocial.com/@realDonaldTrump/posts/114715950565535905; Ryan J. Reilly, "Trump Posts on Social Media Calling for a Special Prosecutor to Investigate the 2020 Election," *NBC News*, June 20, 2025, https://www.nbcnews.com/politics/justice-department/trump-posts-social-media-calling-special-prosecutor-investigate-2020-e-rcna214099.

28. *Ballots being shipped*: Donald J. Trump (@realDonaldTrump), "What's worse, the NBA Players cheating at cards, and probably much else, or the Democrats cheating on Elections. The 2020 Presidential Election, being Rigged and Stolen, is a far bigger SCANDAL. Look what happened to our Country when a Crooked Moron became our 'President!' We now know everything. I hope the DOJ pursues this with as…," Truth Social, October 26, 2025, https://truthsocial.com/@realDonaldTrump/posts/115441871289276790.

28. *Unconstitutional Redistricting Vote*: Donald J. Trump (@realDonaldTrump), "The Unconstitutional Redistricting Vote in California is a GIANT SCAM in that the entire process, in particular the Voting itself, is RIGGED. All 'Mail-In' Ballots, where the Republicans in that State are 'Shut Out,' is under very serious legal and criminal review. STAY TUNED!," Truth Social, November 4, 2025, https://truthsocial.com/@realDonaldTrump/posts/115492361756063244.

28. *and knew he had*: Nadine Yousif, "Bill Barr says Donald Trump 'knew well he lost the election,'" *BBC*, August 3, 2023, https://www.bbc.com/news/world-us-canada-66388176; David Bauder and Jennifer Peltz, "Fox chair Murdoch says 2020 election was fair: court filings," *AP News*, March 7, 2023, https://apnews.com/article/fox-trump-election-claims-defamation-voting-machines-91d6c6e7d39083b7732787e013bb1fc4; Walter Olson, "Trump's 2020 Stolen Election Claims Are Wrong on the Merits," Cato Institute, September 16, 2024, https://www.cato.org/blog/trumps-2020-stolen-election-claims-are-wrong-merits; Thomas B. Griffith et al., "Telling the Truth about the 2020 Election," *National Review*, July 22, 2022, https://www.nationalreview.com/2022/07/telling-the-truth-about-the-2020-election/; Brad Raffensperger, "Trump Recycles Tired 2020 Election Allegations," *National Review*, January 17, 2024, https://www.nationalreview.com/2024/01/trump-recycles-tired-2020-election-allegations/; Ian Hanchett, "Barr: Trump 'Knew Well' He Lost in 2020," *Breitbart*, August 2, 2023, https://www.breitbart.com/clips/2023/08/02/barr-trump-knew-well-he-lost-in-2020/; Byron Tau and Sara Randazzo, "Trump Cries Voter Fraud. In Court, His Lawyers Don't.," *Wall Street Journal*, November 13, 2020, https://www.wsj.com/politics/elections/trump-cries-election-fraud-in-court-his-lawyers-dont-11605271267; *Eastman v. Thompson*, 636 F. Supp. 3d 1078, 1092 (C.D. Cal. 2022); *United States v. Trump*, 753 F. Supp. 3d 17, 40–41 (D.D.C. 2024); *United States v. Trump*, 88 F.4th 990, 996–97 (D.C. Cir. 2023).

28. *admitted the loss privately*: Maanvi Singh, "Trump privately admitted he lost 2020 election, top aides testify," *Guardian*, October 13, 2022, https://www.theguardian.com/us-news/2022/oct/13/trump-admission-election-aides-january-6-panel.

28. *use if he lost*: Jonathan Swan, "Scoop: Trump's plan to declare premature victory," *Axios*, November 1, 2020, https://www.axios.com/2020/11/01/trump-claim -election-victory-ballots; Adam Gabbatt and Hugo Lowell, "'Game Over': Steve Bannon Audio Reveals Trump Planned to Claim Early Victory," *Guardian*, July 14, 2022, https://www.theguardian.com/us-news/2022/jul/14/steve-bannon -audio-trump-declare-victory; Dan Friedman, "New Evidence Shows How Trump Planned to Falsely Declare Victory and Steal the Election," *Mother Jones*, October 13, 2022, https://www.motherjones.com/politics/2022/10/january-6 -committee-trump-falsely-declare-victory/; Jack Smith, Special Counsel, *Final Report on the Special Counsel's Investigations and Prosecutions* (2025), 38–39, https://www.justice.gov/storage/Report-of-Special-Counsel-Smith-Volume-1 -January-2025.pdf.

29. *Trump's senior lawyers*: H.R. Rep. 117-663, at 378, 381–82 (2022), https://www .govinfo.gov/content/pkg/GPO-J6-REPORT/pdf/GPO-J6-REPORT.pdf;   Luke Broadwater and Alan Feuer, "Panel Suggests Trump Knew He Lost the Election, Eyeing Criminal Case," *New York Times*, March 3, 2022, https://www.nytimes .com/2022/03/03/us/politics/trump-jan-6-criminal-case.html.

29. *the claim was bullshit*: H.R. Rep. 117-663 at 378; Susan B. Glasser, "Bill Barr Calls 'Bullshit' on Trump's Election Lies," *New Yorker*, June 13, 2022, https: //www.newyorker.com/news/letter-from-bidens-washington/bill-barr-calls -bullshit-on-trumps-election-lies.

29. *no such evidence*: Indictment at 13, *United States v. Trump*, 704 F. Supp. 3d 196 (D.D.C. 2023) (No. 23-257), https://www.justice.gov/storage/US_v_Trump_23 _cr_257.pdf; Meridith McGraw, "Trump's election fraud claims were false. Here are his advisors who said so.," *Politico*, June 13, 2022, https://www.politico .com/news/2022/06/13/trumps-election-fraud-claims-were-false-here-are -his-advisers-who-said-so-00039346.

29. *most secure in American history*: H.R. Rep. 117-663, at 217; Scott Pelley, "Fired director of U.S. cyber agency Chris Krebs explains why President Trump's claims of election interference are false," *CBS News*, November 30, 2020, https://www.cbsnews.com/news/election-results-security-chris-krebs-60 -minutes-2020-11-29/.

29. *his own bespoke executive order*: Ibid.; "Addressing Risks from Chris Krebs and Government Censorship," The White House, April 9, 2025, https://www .whitehouse.gov/presidential-actions/2025/04/addressing-risks-from-chris -krebs-and-government-censorship/.

30. *for him to prevail*: Indictment at 15, *United States v. Trump*, 704 F. Supp. 3d 196 (No. 23-257); Smith, *Final Report*, at 9–10; Michael D. Shear and Stephanie Saul, "Trump, in Taped Call, Pressured Georgia Official to 'Find' Votes to Overturn Election," *New York Times*, May 26, 2021, https://www.nytimes.com/2021/01/03 /us/politics/trump-raffensperger-call-georgia.html. Smith later repeated this and other conclusions about Trump's conduct in his testimony before Congress, https://www.youtube.com/watch?v=lR-bhPzQYUE.

30. *lost to this f'in guy*: Smith, *Final Report*, at 39; Julia Shapero, "Trump privately admitted he lost election to Biden: Ex-White House aide," *Axios*, June 19, 2022, https://www.axios.com/2022/06/19/trump-admitted-election-alyssa-farah.

30. *believe that their ticket won*: Indictment at 7, *United States v. Trump*, 704 F. Supp. 3d 196 (No. 23-257); Smith, *Final Report*, at 4; David Klepper, "Pence, Trump lawyer clash over what Trump told his vice president ahead of Jan. 6," *PBS News*, August 6, 2023, https://www.pbs.org/newshour/politics/pence-trump -lawyer-clash-over-what-trump-told-his-vice-president-ahead-of-jan-6.

31. *none has been forthcoming*: Recently, the federal government has caused to be unsealed an FBI affidavit in support of a search warrant for Fulton County, GA, 2020 election ballots. The court issued the search warrant, meaning that based on what the government set forth in the FBI affidavit, the court found probable cause that there would be evidence of a crime in the specified items to be searched. The court was not asked to conclude, and the FBI affidavit did not allege, that there was outcome-determinative fraud in either the GA 2020 election for president or the national 2020 election. As is typical in a request for a search warrant, the court did not have the benefit of hearing from any other party at that time, only from the government. Since the issuance and execution of the search warrant, Fulton County has challenged the issuance of the warrant, alleging it omitted substantial contrary evidence. At the time of writing that litigation is pending and it, as well as subsequent evidence, may substantiate, or not, the government's allegations in support of the warrant.

31. *votes the next day*: Maggie Haberman, "Pence Says Trump Pushed Him 'Essentially to Overturn the Election,'" *New York Times*, August 3, 2023, https://www .nytimes.com/2023/08/03/us/politics/pence-trump-election-jan-6.html.

31. *the power to act*: Maggie Haberman and Annie Karni, "Pence Said to Have Told Trump He Lacks Power to Change Election Result," *New York Times*, January 5, 2021, https://www.nytimes.com/2021/01/05/us/politics/pence-trump-election-results.html.

31. *the very next day*: Ibid.; Chris Cameron, "These Are the People Who Died in Connection With the Capitol Riot," *New York Times*, January 5, 2022, https: //www.nytimes.com/2022/01/05/us/politics/jan-6-capitol-deaths.html.

31. *in a lengthy speech*: Full speech available here https://rollcall.com/factbase/trump/ transcript/donald-trump-speech-campaign-rally-the-ellipse-january-6-2021/

31. *never concede*: Brian Naylor, "Read Trump's Jan. 6 Speech, A Key Part Of Impeachment Trial," *NPR*, February 10, 2021, https://www.npr.org/2021/02/10/ 966396848/read-trumps-jan-6-speech-a-key-part-of-impeachment-trial.

31. *have a country anymore*: Naylor, "Trump's Jan. 6 Speech."

32. *built up their expectations*: "Rioters chant 'Hang Mike Pence' on Jan. 6, 2021," *Washington Post*, June 16, 2022, https://www.washingtonpost.com/video /politics/rioters-chant-hang-mike-pence-on-jan-6-2021/2022/06/16/3cc093f1 -0eb7-427d-8073-b5874ca27e80_video.html.

32. *the January 6 insurrection*: Indictment at 36–42, *United States v. Trump*, 704 F. Supp. 3d. 196 (D.D.C. 2023) (No. 23-257), available at https://www.justice.gov /storage/US_v_Trump_23_cr_257.pdf.

32. *charged with protecting the building*: Ryan J. Reilly, "For Jan. 6 rioters who believed Trump, storming the Capitol made sense," *NBC News*, June 20, 2022, https://www .nbcnews.com/politics/donald-trump/jan-6-rioters-believed-trump-storming -capitol-made-sense-rcna33125; Peter Baker and Sabrina Tavernise, "One Legacy of Impeachment: The Most Complete Account So Far of Jan. 6," *New York*

Times, February 13, 2021, https://www.nytimes.com/2021/02/13/us/politics/capitol-riots-impeachment-trial.html.

32. *receive presidential pardons*: Max Matza, "Proud Boys and Oath Keepers among over 1,500 Capitol riot defendants pardoned by Trump," *BBC*, January 20, 2025, https://www.bbc.com/news/articles/c5y7l47xrpko.

33. *a toxic combination of actions*: "Judge grants dismissal of Jan. 6 Case against Trump," *NPR*, November 25, 2024, https://www.npr.org/2024/11/25/nx-s1 -5205376/jan-6-trump-case. Garland's overly cautious approach collided headlong with Trump's strategy of "block and delay" and the Supreme Court's refusal to expedite appellate review to prevent the January 6 case from ever going to trial. See: Glenn Thrush and Adam Goldman, "Inside Garland's Effort to Prosecute Trump," *New York Times*, March 27, 2024, https://www.nytimes .com/2024/03/22/us/politics/trump-jan-6-merrick-garland.html; "Smith urges 'immediate review' of Trump's immunity claims," *SCOTUSblog*, December 21, 2023, https://www.scotusblog.com/2023/12/smith-urges-immediate-review-of -trumps-immunity-claims/. When Richard Nixon asserted executive privilege in response to a subpoena for tape recordings of his conversations in the Watergate case, the Supreme Court bypassed the court of appeals and issued a decision within two months of the government's request for review. See: *United States v. Nixon*, 418 U.S. 683, 683, 690 (1974). In contrast, it took the Court more than two hundred days to issue a decision in the January 6 case from the time the government first sought Supreme Court review. See: "Smith urges 'immediate review,'" *SCOTUSblog*. For more on the Justice Department's delays, see: Part Two of Carol Leonnig and Aaron C. Davis, *Injustice: How Politics and Fear Vanquished America's Justice Department* (New York: Penguin, 2025).

34. *such a lie is not illegal*: Indictment at 2, *United States v. Trump*, 704 F. Supp. 3d 196 (No. 23-257).

34. *the Supreme Court in* Fischer v. United States: *Fischer v. United States*, 603 U.S. 480, 498 (2024).

34. *innumerable other contexts*: 18 U.S.C. §§ 1001, 1344, 1621–23.

35. *devastating consequences*: Aaron Frank, "Kellyanne Conway says Donald Trump's team has 'Alternative Facts.' Which pretty much says it all.," *Washington Post*, January 22, 2017, https://www.washingtonpost.com/news/the-fix/wp/2017 /01/22/kellyanne-conway-says-donald-trumps-team-has-alternate-facts -which-pretty-much-says-it-all/.

Chapter 2

37. *Republicans say the same*: Rachel Weiner et al., "Republican loyalty to Trump, rioters climbs in 3 years after Jan. 6 attack," *Washington Post*, January 2, 2024, https://www.washingtonpost.com/dc-md-va/2024/01/02/jan-6-poll-post -trump/.

37. *has rejected it*: Daniel Barnes, "How Trump's challenges to the 2020 election unfolded in the courtroom," *NBC News*, November 2, 2024, https://www .nbcnews.com/politics/2024-election/trumps-challenges-2020-election -unfolded-courtroom-rcna175490.

37. *with Ms. Lewinsky*: "Testing of a President: Excerpts from Clinton's Grand Jury Testimony as Quoted in Starr's Report to Congress," *New York Times*,

September 17, 1998, https://www.nytimes.com/1998/09/17/us/testing-president
-excerpts-clinton-s-grand-jury-testimony-quoted-starr-s-report.html.
Clinton's statements were subject to legal sanctions because he made them under
oath in a civil deposition in the Paula Jones case, and allegedly in his grand jury
testimony, but not because he repeated the misrepresentations to the public.

37. *I am not a crook*: "'I Am Not A Crook': How A Phrase Got A Life Of Its
Own," *All Things Considered* (*NPR*), November 17, 2013, https://www.npr.org
/2013/11/17/245830047/i-am-not-a-crook-how-a-phrase-got-a-life-of-its-own.

38. *patriots and political prisoners*: Max Matza, "Proud Boys and Oath Keepers
among over 1,500 Capitol riot defendants pardoned by Trump," *BBC*, January
21, 2025, https://www.bbc.com/news/articles/c5y7l47xrpko.

38. *representative democracy survive*: Peter Baker and Sabrina Tavernise, "One
Legacy of Impeachment: The Most Complete Account So Far of Jan. 6," *New York
Times*, February 13, 2021, https://www.nytimes.com/2021/02/13/us/politics
/capitol-riots-impeachment-trial.html.

38. *root and branch*: Matza, "Pardoned by Trump."

38. *grave national injustice*: Ibid.

38. *Proud Boys and Oath Keepers*: Ibid.

39. *by a later administration*: Ella Lee, "Judges who oversaw Jan. 6 cases push back
on Trump pardons," *The Hill*, January 22, 2025, https://thehill.com/regulation
/court-battles/5100754-judge-jan-6-pardons-case-dismissal/.

39. *nonviolent J6 offenders*: Alexandra Marquez and Alex Tabet, "JD Vance says
violent Jan. 6 rioters shouldn't receive pardons," *NBC News*, January 12, 2025,
https://www.nbcnews.com/politics/politics-news/jd-vance-violent-jan-6
-rioters-shouldnt-receive-pardons-rcna187329; Katherine Fung, "AG Pick
Pam Bondi Will Advise Trump on Pardoning January 6 Rioters," *Newsweek*,
January 15, 2025, https://www.newsweek.com/ag-pick-pam-bondi-will-advise
-trump-pardoning-j6-rioters-2015424.

39. *no MAGA left behind*: Aaron Blake, "'No MAGA left behind': Trump's pardons
get even more political," *CNN*, May 28, 2025, https://www.cnn.com/2025/05/28
/politics/analysis-trump-pardons-politics; Paula Reid, "Ed Martin, in his new
role after US attorney nomination fizzled, is reaching out to witnesses in DOJ
weaponization probes," *CNN*, May 28, 2025, https://www.cnn.com/2025/05/28
/politics/ed-martin-justice-department.

39. *former hometown of New York City*: Michael R. Sisak et al., "Guilty: Trump
becomes first former US president convicted of felony crimes," *AP News*, May
31, 2024, https://apnews.com/article/trump-trial-deliberations-jury-testimony
-verdict-85558c6d08efb434d05b694364470aa0.

40. *peacefully transitioning power*: *United States v. Banuelos*, 763 F. Supp. 3d 1, 2
(D.D.C. 2025).

41. *moved to dismiss certain charges*: Tom Dresibach, "Justice Department broadens
Jan. 6 pardons to cover gun, drug-related charges," *NPR*, February 20, 2025, https:
//www.npr.org/2025/02/20/nx-s1-5304454/jan-6-pardons-drugs-firearms.

41. *She noted that DOJ's reasoning*: *United States v. Wilson*, No. 25-cv-545, 2025 WL
1009047, at *7 (D.D.C. March 13, 2025).

41. *based on the J6 pardons*: Ibid., *8–9.

41. *by a new pardon*: Alanna Durkin Richer and Chris Megerian, "Trump pardons Jan. 6 rioter for gun offense and woman convicted of threatening to shoot FBI agents," Associated Press, November 15, 2025, https://apnews.com/article/daniel-edwin-wilson-pardon-trump-capitol-riot-fdd10aaab22a8996a097704bea37b6ae.

41. *worked on the J6 cases*: Adam Goldman et al., "Trump Officials Fire Jan. 6 Prosecutors and Plan Possible F.B.I. Purge," *New York Times*, January 31, 2025, https://www.nytimes.com/2025/01/31/us/politics/trump-fbi-agents.html.

41. *adverse personnel action*: Ibid.

41. *To add to the mendacity*: Ryan Lucas, "Trump official targeting Jan. 6 investigators worked on those cases himself," *NPR*, February 12, 2025, https://www.npr.org/2025/02/12/g-s1-48193/trump-doj-january-6-cases.

42. *innocent J6 defendants*: Specifically, Bove labeled the prosecutions, and federal law enforcement officials' participation in the prosecutions, as a "grave national injustice." See: Memorandum from Emil Bove, Acting Deputy Attorney General, to Brian Driscoll, Acting Director of the Federal Bureau of Investigation 1 (January 31, 2025), https://www.warner.senate.gov/public/_cache/files/8/5/8590fa4b-e135-4ea5-b76f-0f13c097a489/57173F5183F4632CC51D21798D2BEB945EE70C717140FA62CABC283B83D628A9.memorandum-from-the-acting-deputy-attorney-general-01.31.25.pdf.

42. *fired without cause*: Eric Tucker and Alanna Durkin Richer, "Justice Dept. fires more prosecutors, support staff involved in Trump prosecutions, AP Sources Say," *AP News*, July 12, 2025, https://apnews.com/article/jack-smith-justice-department-fired-trump-af94503d10143f5464559fb503425f4f.

42. *target on their backs*: Jack Smith, "The State of the United States: A Conversation with Jack Smith," moderated by Andrew Weissmann, October 14, 2025, University College London Faculty of Laws, *YouTube*, 1:16:41, https://www.youtube.com/watch?v=DR79GW6SvxE.

42. *training and expertise*: Rebecca Beitsch, "FBI purges top officials, agents who worked on Trump's criminal cases," *The Hill*, January 31, 2025, https://thehill.com/homenews/administration/5119963-trump-administration-forces-out-fbi-officials/.

42. *Charlie Kirk assassination*: Ryan J. Reilly and Victoria Ebner, "Kash Patel defends handling of Charlie Kirk investigation and FBI firings in fiery hearing," *NBC News*, September 16, 2025, https://www.nbcnews.com/politics/justice-department/kash-patel-congress-hearing-charlie-kirk-assassination-fbi-rcna231398.

42. *fired by FBI Director Kash Patel*: Glenn Thrush and Alan Feuer, "A 'Broken' Trust: F.B.I. Agents Fired by Patel Speak Out," *New York Times*, September 16, 2025, https://www.nytimes.com/2025/09/16/us/politics/kash-patel-fired-fbi-agents.html. At his confirmation hearing Patel said there would not be political retribution under his leadership, and has denied that the terminations are political retribution.

42. *dying of cancer*: Ibid.

42. *shortly before Giardina's firing*: Ibid.

43. *back up the epithet*: Donald J. Trump (@realDonaldTrump), "Former FBI Agent Walter Giardina is a DIRTY COP! He should be, along with Deranged Jack Smith, the sinister team of Lisa Monaco and Andrew Weissmann, Liddle' Jay

Bratt, Norm Eisen and his FAKE Charity, CREW, Christopher Wray, Merrick Garland, Thomas Windom, who dreamt up the corrupt J-6 Witch Hunt, should be investigated," Truth Social, October 29, 2025, https://truthsocial.com /@realDonaldTrump/posts/115459446440286252.

43. *were themselves fired*: Thrush and Feuer, "A 'Broken' Trust."

43. *The firing and denigration of the public servants who worked on the J6 cases*: In his email of February 5, 2025 Emil Bove provided his justification for the firings: "No FBI employee who simply followed orders and carried out their duties in an ethical manner with respect to January 6 investigations is at risk of termination or other penalties. The only individuals who should be concerned about the process initiated by my January 31, 2025 memo are those who acted with corrupt or partisan intent, who blatantly defied orders from Department leadership, or who exercised discretion in weaponizing the FBI."

43. *Trump was a party*: Sophie Tatum and Jim Acosta, "Report: Trump continues to question Obama's birth certificate," *CNN*, November 29, 2017, https://www.cnn .com/2017/11/28/politics/donald-trump-barack-obama-birth-certificate -nyt; Brent Kendall, "Trump Says Judge's Mexican Heritage Presents 'Absolute Conflict,'" *Wall Street Journal*, June 3, 2016, https://www.wsj.com/articles /donald-trump-keeps-up-attacks-on-judge-gonzalo-curiel-1464911442.

44. *rapists from other countries*: "'Drug dealers, criminals, rapists': What Trump thinks of Mexicans," *BBC*, August 31, 2016, https://www.bbc.com/news/av/world -us-canada-37230916.

44. *than native-born Americans*: Jasmine Garsd, "Immigrants are less likely to commit crimes than U.S.-born Americans, studies find," *NPR*, March 8, 2024, https://www.npr.org/2024/03/08/1237103158/immigrants-are-less-likely-to -commit-crimes-than-us-born-americans-studies-find.

44. *rate for property crimes*: "Undocumented Immigrant Offending Rate Lower Than U.S.-Born Citizen Rate," *National Institute of Justice*, September 12, 2024, https://docs. house.gov/meetings/JU/JU01/20250122/117827/HHRG-119-JU01-20250122-SD004.pdf.

44. *Tren de Aragua*: "Invocation of the Alien Enemies Act Regarding the Invasion of The United States by Tren De Aragua," The White House, March 15, 2025, https:// www.whitehouse.gov/presidential-actions/2025/03/invocation-of-the-alien -enemies-act-regarding-the-invasion-of-the-united-states-by-tren-de-aragua/.

44. *One federal judge thought*: W.M.M. v. Trump, No. 25-10534, 2025 WL 2508869, at *7 (D.D.C. September 2, 2025).

44. *without a hearing*: W.M.M. v. Trump, 154 F.4th 207, 211–12 229 (5th Cir. 2025). The opinion was vacated after the Fifth Circuit Court of Appeals granted the government's motion for rehearing en banc. See: W.M.M. v. Trump, 154 F.4th 319, 321 (5th Cir. 2025).

45. *engaged in an invasion*: Sanchez-Puentes v. Garite, 780 F. Supp. 3d 682, 687 (W.D. Tex. 2025).

45. *married to his wife*: Ibid., 702–3.

45. *judicial process whatsoever*: Laura Romero, "'I feel totally traumatized': Unaccompanied minors from Guatemala describe attempted deportation," *ABC News*, September 3, 2025, https://abcnews.go.com/US/feel-totally-traumatized -unaccompanied-minors-guatemala-describe-attempted/story?id=125233238.

45. *middle of the night*: Ibid.

45. *bound for Guatemala*: Ibid.

45. *their due process rights: Noem v. Abrego Garcia*, 604 U.S. ___, (2025).

45. *to remove children*: 8 U.S.C. § 1232.

46. *what ICE was doing*: Laura Romero and Armando Garcia, "Judge blocks deportation of 76 Guatemalan minors after questioning government's argument," *ABC News*, August 31, 2025, https://abcnews.go.com/Politics/lawyers-block-trump-administration-repatriating-guatemalan-minors/story?id=125140049.

46. *held an immediate hearing*: Ibid.

46. *parents had requested*: Jordan Rubin, "Trump-appointed judge says administration's court claim 'crumbled like a house of cards,'" *MSNBC*, September 19, 2025, https://www.msnbc.com/deadline-white-house/deadline-legal-blog/trump-judge-send-children-guatemala-immigration-rcna232405.

46. *abused her as a child*: Declaration of L.G.M.L. at 1, *L.G.M.L. v. Noem*, No. 25-2942, 2025 WL 2671690 (D.D.C. September 18, 2025).

46. *had been requested: L.G.M.L. v. Noem*, 2025 WL 2671690, at *3.

46. *parents at their own request*: Ibid., *4.

47. *resolved at a hearing*: Chiara Eisner, "Hundreds of unaccompanied Guatemalan children can stay in the U.S. for now, judge says," *NPR*, August 31, 2025, https://www.npr.org/2025/08/31/nx-s1-5524312/federal-judge-block-guatemalan-children-deportation.

47. *on X that day*: Stephen Miller (@StephenM), "The Biden judge is effectively kidnapping these migrant children and refusing to let them return home to their parents in their home country," X, August 31, 2025, https://x.com/StephenM/status/1962265343679717528.

47. *in his first term*: Rubin, "Trump-Appointed Judge."

47. *consent of the parents*: Ibid.

48. *come back to Guatemala: L.G.M.L. v. Noem*, 2025 WL 2671690, at *1, *16.

48. *did not know about it*: Ibid., *5.

48. *alerted the public*: Emily Green et al., "Exclusive: Guatemalan Document Undercuts U.S. Claims on Child Deportations," Reuters, September 3, 2025, https://www.reuters.com/legal/government/guatemalan-document-undercuts-us-claims-child-deportations-2025-09-03/.

48. *just days earlier: L.G.M.L. v. Noem*, 2025 WL 2671690, at *5, *16.

49. *dreaded cancerous tumor*: Ginger Gibson, "Trump says immigrants are 'poisoning the blood of our country.' Biden campaign likens comments to Hitler.," *NBC News*, December 17, 2023, https://www.nbcnews.com/politics/2024-election/trump-says-immigrants-are-poisoning-blood-country-biden-campaign-liken-rcna130141.

49. *sent him to El Salvador*: Cristian Farias, "The U.S. Government's Extraordinary Pursuit of Kilmar Ábrego García," *New Yorker*, September 15, 2025, https://www.newyorker.com/news/the-lede/the-us-governments-extraordinary-pursuit-of-kilmar-abrego-garcia.

49. *retribution if he were sent there*: Ibid.

49. *prospect for release*: Ibid.

50. *Once Abrego Garcia was stashed*: Dareh Gregorian et al., "Trump claims he 'could' have Kilmar Abrego Garcia returned to the U.S. His administration

has said otherwise," *NBC News*, April 30, 2025, https://www.nbcnews.com
/politics/justice-department/trump-claims-kilmar-abrego-garcia-returned
-us-administration-said-othe-rcna203734.

50. *hundreds of thousands of dollars*: Ibid. It later came to light that Secretary of
State Marco Rubio apparently had gained access to CECOT by promising
to send nine MS-13 gang leaders in US custody back to El Salvador, despite
the fact that some of them were informants under the US government's
protection. See: John Hudson et al., "Rubio promised to betray U.S. informants
to get Trump's El Salvador prison deal," *Washington Post*, October 19, 2025,
https://www.washingtonpost.com/national-security/2025/10/19/rubio-el
-salvador-prison-bukele-ms13-informants/.

50. *lie to the court*: Scott Pelley et al., "Fired Justice Department lawyer says he refused
to lie in the Abrego Garcia case," *CBS News*, October 19, 2025, https://www
.cbsnews.com/news/erez-reuveni-justice-department-whistleblower-kilmar
-abrego-garcia-60-minutes/.

50. *he was a career lawyer*: Ibid.

50. *he was promptly fired*: Ibid.

50. *besmirch Abrego Garcia herself*: Rebecca Beitsch, "Bondi says mistakenly deported
man 'not coming back to our country,'" *The Hill*, April 16, 2025, https://thehill.com
/homenews/administration/5251491-pam-bondi-kilmar-abrego-garcia-return/.

51. *overseeing the case*: *Abrego Garcia v. Noem*, No. 25-1404, 2025 WL 1135112, at *1
(4th Cir. April 17, 2025).

52. *remove Abrego Garcia from the country*: Ibid.

52. *he bluntly penned*: *Abrego Garcia v. Noem*, No. 25-1345, 2025 WL 1021113, at *6
(4th Cir. April 7, 2025) (Wilkinson, J., concurring).

52. *what was wrong, right*: *Abrego Garcia v. Noem*, 2025 WL 1135112, at *1.

52. *duty to the court*: *Abrego Garcia v. Noem*, 2025 WL 1021113, at *3 n.4 (Thatcher,
J., concurring).

52. *officers of the court*: Ibid.

53. *still hold dear*: *Abrego Garcia v. Noem*, 2025 WL 1135112, at *1.

53. *path of perfect lawlessness*: *Abrego Garcia v. Noem*, 2025 WL 1021113, at *7
(Wilkinson, J., concurring).

53. *there is still time*: *Abrego Garcia v. Noem*, 2025 WL 1135112, at *3.

53. *headline about the case*: The White House (@WhiteHouse), "Fixed it for you,
@NYTimes. Oh, and by the way, @ChrisVanHollen — he's NOT coming back,"
X, April 18, 2025, https://x.com/WhiteHouse/status/1913241658579440126
?lang=en.

53. *Never Coming Back*: Ibid. The government's misbehavior, including flouting
court orders, infliction of needless pain on Abrego Garcia, and potential
vindictive prosecution, are recounted in decisions by the federal judges
overseeing his civil and criminal cases. *United States v. Abrego*, No. 3:25-CR-
00115, 2025 WL 2814712, at *1 (M.D. Tenn. Oct. 3, 2025); *Abrego Garcia v. Noem*,
No. 8:25-CV-02780-PX, 2025 WL 3545447, at *1 (D. Md. Dec. 11, 2025).

54. *at least our blue cities*: Juliana Kim, "Trump says National Guard will soon go
to New Orleans. Here's the latest," *NPR*, October 16, 2025, https://www.npr
.org/2025/10/10/nx-s1-5567177/national-guard-map-chicago-california-oregon;

Ryan Goodman et al., "The 'Presumption of Regularity' in Trump Administration Litigation," *Just Security*, November 20, 2025, https://www.justsecurity.org /120547/presumption-regularity-trump-administration-litigation/.

54. *normal law enforcement efforts*: Kat Lonsdorf and Ayesha Rascoe, "Trump wants to send troops to 'war-ravaged' Portland. City officials say there's no need," *NPR*, September 28, 2025, https://www.npr.org/2025/09/28/nx-s1-5555496/trump -wants-to-send-troops-to-war-ravaged-portland-city-officials-say-theres-no-need.

54. *call in the marines*: Alicia Victoria Lozano et al., "Judge rules Trump illegally deployed National Guard and Marines to Los Angeles," *NBC News*, September 2, 2025, https://www.nbcnews.com/news/us-news/judge-rules-trump-illegally -deployed-national-guard-l-rcna224779.

54. *And the national guard*: Ibid.

54. *untethered to the facts*: Oregon v. Trump, No. 3:25-cv-1756-IM, 2025 WL 2817646, at *11 (D. Or. October 4, 2025). Another federal judge in Chicago found that senior Border Patrol official Gregory Bovino lied about being hit in the head with a rock before deploying tear gas. See: Priscilla Alvarez, "Federal judge says border patrol chief admitted he lied, in ruling limiting federal agents' use of force in Chicago," *CNN*, November 7, 2025, https://www.cnn.com/2025/11/06 /us/gregory-bovino-deposition-chicago-immigration.

54. *favor to any party*: Mark Berman and Derek Hawkins, "Judge temporarily blocks Trump from deploying troops in Portland," *Washington Post*, October 4, 2025, https://www.washingtonpost.com/politics/2025/10/04/trump-portland -oregon-national-guard/.

55. *This did not prevent*: Aaron Blake, "The White House claims a left-wing judicial 'insurrection.' But many GOP and Trump nominees are rebuking the president, too," *CNN*, October 6, 2025, https://www.cnn.com/2025/10/06/politics /republican-federal-judges-trump.

55. *on these judges*: Avery Lotz and Andrew Pantazi, "DOJ's No. 2 frames legal fight as 'war' on judges, state bars," *Axios*, November 9, 2025, https://www.axios .com/2025/11/09/doj-blanche-war-activist-judges-dc-bar-associations.

55. *Lies abound*: Daniel Dale and Tara Subramaniam, "Fact check: Breaking down Trump's 654 false claims over 14 weeks during the coronavirus pandemic," *CNN*, May 29, 2020, https://www.cnn.com/2020/05/29/politics/fact-check -trump-coronavirus-pandemic-dishonesty; Bryan Naylor, "Trump Walks Back Controversial Comments On Russian Election Interference," *NPR*, July 17, 2018, https://www.npr.org/2018/07/17/629764949/ryan-vladimir-putin-does-not -share-our-interests; Charles Lister, "Trump Says ISIS Is Defeated. Reality Says Otherwise.," *Politico*, March 18, 2019, https://www.politico.com/magazine /story/2019/03/18/trump-isis-terrorists-defeated-foreign-policy-225816/.

55. *the disregard of international law*: On the legal issues involving the seizure of President Maduro, see Marko Milanovic, "Some Further Thoughts on the Illegal US Attack on Venezuela: Self-Defence, Cyber, and Continuing Coercion," *EJIL:Talk!: Blog of the European Journal of International Law*, January 7, 2026, https://www.ejiltalk.org/some-further-thoughts-on-the-illegal-us-attack -on-venezuela-self-defence-cyber-and-continuing-coercion/; and on the general legal consensus of the United States military attack on Venezuela, see Michael

Schmitt, Tess Bridgeman and Ryan Goodman, "Operation Southern Spear: Why the Crews, Drugs, and Boats are Not Targetable," *Just Security,* December 7, 2025, https://www.justsecurity.org/126553/operation-southern-spear-international-law/ ("The administration has claimed that the operations against the drug cartels are occurring in the context of a non-international armed conflict [NIAC] that triggers the applicability of LOAC. This assertion is unambiguously incorrect as a matter of law, a point illustrated by the near universal rejection of it among LOAC experts.").

56. *health of the entire nation*: Meg Tirrell, "HHS employees demand RFK Jr. resign for 'compromising the health of this nation,'" *CNN*, September 3, 2025, https://www.cnn.com/2025/09/03/health/hhs-employees-letter-rfk-jr; "Improving Oversight of Federal Grantmaking," White House, August 7, 2025, https://www.whitehouse.gov/presidential-actions/2025/08/improving-oversight-of-federal-grantmaking/; "Restoring Gold Standard Science," White House, May 23, 2025, https://www.whitehouse.gov/presidential-actions/2025/05/restoring-gold-standard-science/; Jerry Wu et al., "Federal government freezes $790 million in funding for Northwestern," *Daily Northwestern*, April 8, 2025, https://dailynorthwestern.com/2025/04/08/top-stories/federal-government-freezes-790-million-in-funding-for-northwestern/; Jonathan Schwabish and Judah Axelrod, "NSF Has Canceled More Than 1,500 Grants. Nearly 90 Percent Were Related to DEI.," *Urban Institute*, July 9, 2025, https://www.urban.org/urban-wire/nsf-has-canceled-more-1500-grants-nearly-90-percent-were-related-dei; Brian Buntz, "NSF chief quits as DOGE drives 55% budget cut and grant freeze," *R&D World*, April 25, 2025, https://www.rdworldonline.com/nsf-chief-quits-as-doge-drives-55-budget-cut-and-grant-freeze/; Jeffrey Mervis, "In latest blow, National Science Foundation staff to be booted from their headquarters," *Science*, June 25, 2025, https://www.science.org/content/article/latest-blow-national-science-foundation-staff-be-booted-their-headquarters.

56. *disclosing the truth to the court*: Dana L. Gold et al., "Protected Whistleblower Disclosure of Erez Reuveni Regarding Violation of Laws, Rules & Regulations, Abuse of Authority, and Substantial and Specific Danger to Health and Safety at the Department of Justice," June 24, 2025, https://www.judiciary.senate.gov/imo/media/doc/06-24-2025_-_Protected_Whistleblower_Disclosure_of_Erez_Reuveni_Redacted.pdf.

56. *poor economic news*: Nick Niedzwiadek, "Ex-BLS chief said she was blindsided by Trump firing," *Politico*, September 16, 2025, https://www.politico.com/news/2025/09/16/ex-bls-chief-said-she-was-blindsided-by-trump-firing-00567852.

56. *wrong with her calculations*: Ibid.

56. *positive economic news*: Linda Qiu, "For Trump, Data Is Often 'Phony,' Unless It Supports His Views," *New York Times*, September 25, 2025, https://www.nytimes.com/interactive/2025/09/25/us/politics/trump-data-facts.html.

57. *our big number testing*: Jessica McDonald, "Trump Falsely Says COVID-19 Surge 'Only' Due to Testing, Misleads on Deaths," FactCheck.org, June 25, 2020, https://www.factcheck.org/2020/06/trump-falsely-says-covid-19-surge-only-due-to-testing-misleads-on-deaths/.

57. *the honesty crisis*: Ethan Singer, "Thousands of U.S. Government Web Pages Have Been Taken Down Since Friday," *New York Times*, February 3, 2025, https://www.nytimes.com/2025/02/02/upshot/trump-government-websites -missing-pages.html; "Restoring Truth and Sanity to American History," The White House, March 27, 2025, https://www.whitehouse.gov/presidential -actions/2025/03/restoring-truth-and-sanity-to-american-history/; Michael D. Shear and Stephanie Saul, "Trump, in Taped Call, Pressured Georgia Official to 'Find' Votes to Overturn Election," *New York Times*, May 26, 2021, https://www.nytimes. com/2021/01/03/us/politics/trump-raffensperger-call-georgia.html; Ayesha Rascoe, "Who Was On The Trump-Ukraine Call?," *NPR*, November 7, 2019, https:// www.npr.org/2019/11/07/775456663/who-was-on-the-trump-ukraine-call.

58. *had indicted Manafort*: Carrie Johnson and Ryan Lucas, "Paul Manafort Pleads Guilty, Agrees To Cooperate With Mueller's Russia Probe," *NPR*, September 14, 2018, https://www.npr.org/2018/09/14/643073024/paul-manafort -to-plead-guilty-in-agreement-to-avert-a-second-federal-trial.

58. *charges in both indictments*: Ibid.

58. *amount of money involved*: David Smith, "Paul Manafort given seven-year prison term and severe rebuke from judge," *The Guardian*, March 13, 2019, https://www .theguardian.com/us-news/2019/mar/13/paul-manafort-second-sentencing -hearing-donald-trump.

59. *one man can wear*: 190313 Manafort Sentencing Transcript, Document-Cloud, March 13, 2019, 61, https://www.documentcloud.org/documents /6165487-190313-Manafort-Sentencing-Transcript/?q=more+houses&mode =document#document/p61.

59. *lied to the investigators*: Ibid., 77.

59. *democracy can't work*: Ibid., 63.

59. *where facts still matter*: Ibid., 68.

60. *Trump pardoned him*: Smith, "Paul Manafort"; Josh Gerstein, "DOJ: Manafort pardon may affect forfeitures," *Politico*, January 11, 2021, https://www.politico .com/news/2021/01/11/doj-paul-manafort-trump-pardon-457378.

60. *less than two years in prison*: Gerstein, "Manafort Pardon."

Chapter 3

62. *Russian Bolshevik revolution*: Abrams v. United States, 250 U.S. 616, 625–26 (1919) (Holmes, J., dissenting).

62. *competition of the market*: Ibid., 630 (Holmes, J., dissenting).

62. *expand free speech rights*: Nat'l Inst. of Fam. & Life Advocs. v. Becerra, 585 U.S. 755, 772 (2018); Hustler Mag., Inc. v. Falwell, 485 U.S. 46, 51–52 (1988).

63. *Congress has criminalized*: Ali Dukakis and Lucien Bruggeman, "Roger Stone found guilty on all 7 counts," *ABC News*, November 15, 2019, https://abcnews .go.com/Politics/roger-stone-found-guilty-counts/story?id=67015102; C. Ryan Barber and Sadie Gurman, "James Comey Pleads Not Guilty to Charges of Lying to Congress," *Wall Street Journal*, October 8, 2025, https://www.wsj.com /us-news/law/james-comey-federal-court-not-guilty-plea-c35f2522.

63. *by congressional statute*: "Stewart begins serving jail term," *NBC News*, October 8, 2004, https://www.nbcnews.com/id/wbna6205192; Dan Mangan and Kevin

Breuninger, "Former Trump campaign chief Paul Manafort found guilty of bank and tax fraud," *CNBC*, August 21, 2018, https://www.cnbc.com/2018/08/21/paul-manafort-verdict.html.

64. *withholding congressionally appropriated military aid*: Nicholas Fandos and Michael D. Shear, "Trump Impeached for Abuse of Power and Obstruction of Congress," *New York Times*, December 18, 2019, https://www.nytimes.com/2019/12/18/us/politics/trump-impeached.html.

64. *rivals at the time*: Ibid.

64. *Trump took to the airwaves*: Jeremy Diamond, "Trump focuses on 'perfect' Ukraine call despite allegations of broader pressure campaign," *CNN*, November 4, 2019, https://www.cnn.com/2019/11/04/politics/donald-trump-ukraine-perfect-call-defense.

64. *declaration to Congress*: Philip Ewing, "'Not Guilty': Trump Acquitted On 2 Articles Of Impeachment As Historic Trial Closes," *NPR*, February 5, 2020, https://www.npr.org/2020/02/05/801429948/not-guilty-trump-acquitted-on-2-articles-of-impeachment-as-historic-trial-closes.

65. *FBI Director James Comey*: Barber and Gurman, "Comey Pleads Not Guilty."

65. *lawsuit against Rudy Giuliani*: Zoë Richards and Phil Helsel, "Rudy Giuliani satisfies judgment in defamation case brought by former Georgia election workers," *NBC News*, February 24, 2025, https://www.nbcnews.com/politics/politics-news/rudy-giuliani-judgment-defamation-case-former-georgia-election-workers-rcna193581.

65. *election votes in Georgia*: Daniel Barnes and Summer Concepcion, "Rudy Giuliani defamed former Georgia election workers, a federal judge rules," *NBC News*, August 30, 2023, https://www.nbcnews.com/politics/2020-election/judge-rules-rudy-giuliani-defamed-georgia-election-workers-rcna102555.

65. *threats to them both*: Kyle Cheney and Josh Gerstein, "'How evil': Ruby Freeman describes violent threats after false Trump, Giuliani attacks," *Politico*, December 13, 2023, https://www.politico.com/news/2023/12/13/giuliani-trial-ruby-freeman-testimony-00131659.

65. *held him legally responsible*: Richards and Helsel, "Rudy Giuliani Satisfies Judgment."

65. *awarded the women almost $150 million*: Ibid.

65. *even more direct example*: David Bauder et al., "Fox, Dominion reach $787M settlement over election claims," *AP News*, April 18, 2023, https://apnews.com/article/fox-news-dominion-lawsuit-trial-trump-2020-0ac71f75acfacc52ea80b3e747fb0afe.

66. *switch votes to Biden*: Ibid.

66. *thrown the election to Biden*: Meghan Roos, "Dominion Voting Systems 'Categorically Denies' Election Tech Glitches Following Trump Accusations," *Newsweek*, November 13, 2020, https://www.newsweek.com/dominion-voting-systems-categorically-denies-election-tech-glitches-following-trump-accusations-1547405.

66. *Dominion filed a civil case*: All those sued denied any wrongdoing. Rudy Giuliani, Sidney Powell and One American News Network settled their respective cases against Dominion and/or its CEO Eric Coomer for undisclosed amounts. Mike Lindell was found liable to Coomer for $2.3m. At the time of writing, he is challenging that verdict.

66. *its supposed election interference*: Josh Gerstein, "Judge refuses to toss out Dominion defamation suits against Powell, Giuliani and Lindell," *Politico*, August 11, 2021, https://www.politico.com/news/2021/08/11/judge-dominion -defamation-suits-powell-504000; Tierney Sneed and Marshall Cohen, "Far-right network OAN settles 2020 election defamation suit brought by ex-Dominion executive," *CNN*, September 5, 2023, https://www.cnn.com/2023 /09/05/media/dominion-exec-oan-lawsuit-settlement.

66. *just before the scheduled trial*: Bauder et al., "Settlement over Election Claims."

67. *2020 election are true*: US Dominion, Inc. v. Fox News Network, LLC, No. N21C-03-257 EMD, 2023 WL 2730567, at *21 (Del. Super. Ct. March 31, 2023).

67. *spring and the summer*: Ibid., *5.

68. *the courthouse doors*: Certain lies related to elections are prohibited. Lies about when, where, and how to vote are all subject to government prohibition. The people who sent text messages encouraging Hillary Clinton supporters to vote for her by text message, which of course can't be done, were prosecuted. See: Aaron Katersky, "Twitter influencer sentenced for trying to trick Clinton supporters into voting by text," *ABC News*, October 18, 2023, https://abcnews .go.com/US/twitter-influencer-sentenced-trick-clinton-supporters-voting-text /story?id=104096660. Even no-electioneering zones, creating a buffer around voting precincts, have been upheld as appropriate to give voters time and space to vote, without undue pressure or intimidation. See: *Burson v. Freeman*, 504 U.S. 191, 211 (1992). False and misleading speech related to elections is subject to the criminal law, but only if it is speech that serves to interfere with the process of voting. Federal and state laws prohibit voter intimidation, such as advising potential voters that they will be subject to tax audits, immigration consequences, or eviction for exercising the right to vote. These are deemed "true threats" that can be punished by the state to protect the right to vote. See: "Fact Sheet: Regulation of False, Misleading, or Intimidating Speech About Elections," Georgetown Law Institute for Constitutional Advocacy and Protection, https: //www.law.georgetown.edu/icap/wp-content/uploads/sites/32/2024/08/Fact -Sheet-False-Misleading-and-Intimidating-Election-Information.pdf.

   The Supreme Court permits such regulations of speech because the speech unduly interferes with a separate right to vote. "The right to vote freely for the candidate of one's choice is of the essence of a democratic society," said the Court in 1964. See: *Reynolds v. Sims*, 377 U.S. 533, 555 (1964). "No right is more precious in a free country than that of having a voice in the election of those who make the laws under which, as good citizens, we must live. Other rights, even the most basic, are illusory if the right to vote is undermined." See: *Wesberry v. Sanders*, 376 U.S. 1, 17 (1964). The right to vote is a "fundamental political right, because [it is] preservative of all rights." See: *Yick Wo v. Hopkins*, 118 U.S. 356, 370 (1886).

69. *to secure the presidency again*: Rachel Weiner et al., "Republican loyalty to Trump, rioters climbs in 3 years after Jan. 6 attack," *Washington Post*, January 2, 2024, https://www.washingtonpost.com/dc-md-va/2024/01/02/jan-6-poll-post -trump/.

70. *among young viewers*: Mary Randolph and Elisa Shearer, "How the audiences of 30 major news sources differ by age," Pew Research Center, August 28, 2025,

https://www.pewresearch.org/short-reads/2025/08/28/how-the-audiences -of-30-major-news-sources-differ-by-age/.

70. *none at all*: "Social Media and News Fact Sheet," Pew Research Center, September 25, 2025, https://www.pewresearch.org/journalism/fact-sheet/social -media-and-news-fact-sheet/.

70. *social media platforms*: Galen Stocking et al., "America's News Influencers," Pew Research Center, November 18, 2024, https://www.pewresearch.org/journalism /2024/11/18/americas-news-influencers/.

70. *those over 65*: "Social Media and News Fact Sheet," Pew Research Center.

71. *to make a breakthrough*: Will Dahlgreen, "Why are Nobel Prize winners getting older," *BBC*, October 7, 2016, https://www.bbc.com/news/science-environment -37578899; Maja Založnik, "Ageing Nobel Laureates or an Ageing Mankind?," Oxford Institute of Population Ageing, October 12, 2016, https://www.ageing.ox .ac.uk/blog/2016-Zaloznik-Blog-AgeofNobelLaureatesl.

71. *huge and growing backlog*: Alex Young, "Too Much Information: Ineffective Intelligence Collection," *Harvard International Review*, August 18, 2019, https: //hir.harvard.edu/too-much-information/.

71. *people we've never met*: Matteo Cinelli, "The echo chamber effect on social media," *Proceedings of the National Academy of Sciences of the United States of America* 118, no. 9 (2021): 6–7, https://www.pnas.org/doi/epdf/10.1073/pnas .2023301118; Jonathan Haidt, "Why the Past 10 Years of American Life Have Been Uniquely Stupid," *Atlantic*, April 11, 2022, https://www.theatlantic.com/magazine /archive/2022/05/social-media-democracy-trust-babel/629369/.

71. *produce repetitious orthodoxies*: Giuliano da Empoli has cogently described this global phenomenon, and the power that it has conferred on "tech bros." See: Empoli, *The Hour of the Predator: Encounters with the Autocrats and Tech Billionaires Taking Over the World* (London: Pushkin Press, 2025).

72. *to keep track of*: Richard Spencer Childs, "Politics Without Politicians," *Saturday Evening Post*, Jan. 22, 1910, 4–6; Bernard Hirschhorn, "Richard Spencer Childs: The Political Reformer and His Influence on the Work of the American Judicature Society," *Judicature* 73 (1990): 185, Westlaw.

72. *bundles of candidates*: Childs, "Politics Without Politicians," 4–6.

72. *asparagus voting system*: Ibid.; Hirschhorn, "Richard Spencer Childs," 185.

73. *each individual candidate*: Childs, "Politics Without Politicians," 5–6.

73. *busy members of the electorate*: John H. Aldrich, *Why Parties? The Origin and Transformation of Political Parties in America* (Chicago: University of Chicago Press, 1995), 269.

73. *infamous Boss Tweed*: Charles McCarthy, *The Wisconsin Idea* (New York: Macmillan, 1912), 89–90; Daniel J. Moskowitz and Jon C. Rogowski, "Ballot Reform, the Personal Vote, and Political Representation in the United States," *British Journal of Political Science* 54, no. 1 (2024): 37, https://doi.org/10.1017 /S0007123423000091; Denis Tilden Lynch, *"Boss" Tweed* (Livingston, NJ: Trans- action Publishers, 1927); Gur Bligh, "Extremism in the Electoral Arena: Chal- lenging the Myth of American Exceptionalism," *Brigham Young University Law Review* (2008): 1397, Westlaw; Kevin Cofsky, "Pruning the Political Thicket: The Case for Strict Scrutiny of State," *University of Pennsylvania Law Review*

145 (1996) 359 n.22, Westlaw; Mark R. Brown, "Ballot Fees as Impermissible Qualifications for Federal Office," *American University Law Review* 54 (2005): 1296–97, Westlaw.

73. *showing of popular support*: McCarthy, *The Wisconsin Idea*, 88–89; H. Feldman, "The Direct Primary in New York State," *American Political Science Review* 11, no. 3 (1917): 494, https://doi.org/10.2307/1944250; Alan Ware, *The American Direct Primary: Party Institutionalization and Transformation in the North* (Cambridge, UK: Cambridge University Press, 2002), 112, 221 n.25.

73. *minimum number of qualified voters*: Ware, *The American Direct Primary*, 112, 221 n.25; Direct Primary Act of 1903, ch. 451, 1903 Wis. Session Laws 754; *Munro v. Socialist Workers Party*, 479 U.S. 189, 193 (1986); *Jenness v. Fortson*, 403 U.S. 431, 442 (1971).

74. *eminently reasonable*: *Burdick v. Takushi*, 504 U.S. 428, 440 n.10 (1992).

74. *accompany the democratic processes*: Ibid., 433.

74. *Karl Popper envisioned*: Karl Popper, *The Open Society and Its Enemies* (London: Routledge, 1945); Cinelli, "The Echo Chamber Effect," 6–7.

75. *echo-chamber phenomenon*: Cinelli, "The Echo Chamber Effect," 6–7; Neil C. Hughes, "Internet algorithms holding you hostage: how to escape the matrix," *Cybernews*, October 5, 2024, https://cybernews.com/editorial/internet -algorithms-escape-matrix/.

75. *fake with the true*: Christopher Seneca, "How to Break Out of Your Social Media Echo Chamber," *Wired*, September 17, 2020, https://www.wired.com/story /facebook-twitter-echo-chamber-confirmation-bias/.

75. *citizenship and self-government*: Cass Sunstein, *Republic.com* (Princeton, NJ: Princeton University Press, 2001), 123.

75. *creates siloed sheep states*: The argument is not that an individual user cannot overcome the social media constraints to find and evaluate conflicting viewpoints. See: Seneca, "Social Media Echo Chamber." A user can also use the platform and other data to evaluate whether something is true or not. That was true of the "asparagus" voting system, too, of course. The point is what, in practice, this requires of the citizen.

My observations about the anachronistic use of the "marketplace of ideas" metaphor are not unique. Cass Sunstein has written about this issue in *Democracy and the Problem of Free Speech* (New York: Free Press, 1995). He favors the law focusing on how speech promotes or undermines deliberative democracy, as opposed to focusing on protecting a marketplace of ideas in and of itself.

76. *exacerbates this problem*: Steven Lee Myers, "U.S. Bars 5 European Tech Regulators and Researchers," *New York Times*, December 23, 2025, https: //www.nytimes.com/2025/12/23/technology/trump-rubio-european-tech -disinformation-digital-services-act.html. At the same time, the Justice Department has also narrowed enforcement of the Foreign Agents Registration Act; see: Ki Hong et al., "Navigating the Foreign Agents Registration Act's shifting sands: What to make of DOJ's new enforcement priorities," Reuters, April 1, 2025, https://www.reuters.com/legal/legalindustry/navigating-foreign -agents-registration-acts-shifting-sands-what-make-dojs-new-2025-04-01/.

76. *mantle of truth*: Ali Swenson and Christine Fernando, "As social media guardrails fade and AI deepfakes go mainstream, experts warn of impact on

elections," *PBS News*, December 27, 2023, https://www.pbs.org/newshour /politics/as-social-media-guardrails-fade-and-ai-deepfakes-go-mainstream -experts-warn-of-impact-on-elections.

76. *in the image were real*: Juliet Macur, "Trump Has Made Claims About Abrego Garcia's Tattoos. Here's a Closer Look.," *New York Times*, May 8, 2025, https: //www.nytimes.com/2025/05/08/us/kilmar-abrego-garcia-tattoos-ms-13.html.

77. *science regarding vaccines*: Mike Stobbie, "Ousted vaccine panel members say rigorous science is being abandoned under RFK Jr.," *PBS News*, July 30, 2025, https://www.pbs.org/newshour/health/ousted-vaccine-panel-members-say -rigorous-science-is-being-abandoned-under-rfk-jr.

77. *numbers are poor*: Nick Niedzwiadek and Sam Sutton, "Trump fires statistics chief after soft jobs report," *Politico*, August 1, 2025, https://www.politico.com/ news/2025/08/01/trump-firing-bureau-labor-statistics-chief-jobs-report-00488960.

77. *historical weather patterns*: Jeff Brady, "Far more environmental data is being deleted in Trump's second term than before," *NPR*, August 8, 2025, https://www .npr.org/2025/08/08/nx-s1-5495338/climate-change-environment-websites-trump.

77. *country by the government*: Scott Pelley et al., "Fired Justice Department lawyer says he refused to lie in the Abrego Garcia case," *CBS News*, October 19, 2025, https: //www.cbsnews.com/news/erez-reuveni-justice-department-whistleblower -kilmar-abrego-garcia-60-minutes/.

77. *follow court orders*: Dana L. Gold et al., "Protected Whistleblower Disclosure of Erez Reuveni Regarding Violation of Laws, Rules & Regulations, Abuse of Authority, and Substantial and Specific Danger to Health and Safety at the Department of Justice," Government Accountability Project, June 24, 2025, https: //www.judiciary.senate.gov/imo/media/doc/06-24-2025_-_Protected _Whistleblower_Disclosure_of_Erez_Reuveni_Redacted.pdf.

77. *unconstitutional Trump blacklists*: Four judges found the Trump administration's executive orders targeting law firms violated several constitutional provisions; see: *Jenner & Block LLP v. U.S. Department of Justice*, 784 F. Supp. 3d 76, 118 (D.D.C. 2025); *Perkins Coie LLP v. U.S. Department of Justice*, 783 F. Supp. 3d 105, 180 (D.D.C. 2025); *Susman Godfrey LLP v. Executive Office of the President*, 789 F. Supp. 3d 15, 58 (D.D.C. 2025); *Wilmer Cutler Pickering Hale & Dorr LLP v. Executive Office of the President*, 784 F. Supp. 3d 127, 173 (D.D.C. 2025). The Trump administration is appealing these decisions; see: Zach Montague, "Trump Appeals Ruling Blocking Executive Order Against Perkins Coie," *New York Times*, June 30, 2025, https://www.nytimes.com/2025/06/30/us/politics /trump-perkins-coie.html; Abigail Adcox, "Appealing Jenner Ruling, Trump Admin to Fight Second Law Firm EO Case," *Law.com*, July 21, 2025, https: //www.law.com/nationallawjournal/2025/07/21/appealing-jenner-ruling -trump-admin-to-fight-second-law-firm-eo-case/; David Thomas, "Trump Files Appeal to Revive Executive Order Against Law Firm Susman Godfrey," Reuters, August 22, 2025, https://www.reuters.com/legal/government/trump-files-appeal -revive-executive-order-against-law-firm-susman-godfrey-2025-08-22/; Amanda O'Brien and Abigail Adcox, "DOJ Files Appeal in Wilmer Executive Order Case," *Law.com*, July 25, 2025, https://www.law.com/americanlawyer/2025 /07/25/doj-files-appeal-in-wilmer-executive-order-case/.

77. *center in Saint Petersburg*: "Read the Mueller Report: Searchable Document and Index," *New York Times*, April 18, 2019, https://www.nytimes.com/interactive /2019/04/18/us/politics/mueller-report-document.html; Mark Mazzetti, "G.O.P.-Led Senate Panel Details Ties Between 2016 Trump Campaign and Russia," *New York Times*, August 18, 2020, https://www.nytimes.com/2020/08/18/us /politics/senate-intelligence-russian-interference-report.html. Today, China is reportedly harnessing the power of AI to engage in similar propaganda activities. See: Brett J. Goldstein and Brett V. Benson, "The Era of A.I. Propaganda Has Arrived, and America Must Act," *New York Times*, August 5, 2025, https://www .nytimes.com/2025/08/05/opinion/china-ai-propaganda.html.

78. *described as information warfare*: Indictment at 10, *United States v. Internet Rsch. Agency LLC*, No. 1:18-CR-00032, (D.D.C. February 16, 2018).

78. *in the general election*: Ibid., 43.

78. *disillusioned with being sold out*: Ibid., 34.

78. *except Sanders and Trump*: Ibid., 43.

78. *coming from patriotic Americans*: Ibid., 34–36.

78. *hard physical evidence*: Mazzetti, "Senate Panel Details Ties."

78. *signatories on that report*: Ibid.

79. *required such registration*: Indictment at 26, Foreign Agents Registration Act of 1938, Pub. L. 75-483, 52 Stat. 631.

79. *So what is?*: Sunstein and others have devised various possible reforms: "free media time for political candidates, federal guidelines for the coverage of public issues, curtailment of the ability of the wealthy to buy access in the media," to name a few. See: Scott London, review of *Democracy and the Problem of Free Speech*, by Cass Sunstein, in *Scott London* (website), 1996, https://scott.london/reviews /sunstein.html.

Chapter 4

82. *interpret the Constitution*: *Marbury v. Madison*, 5 U.S. (1 Cranch) 137, 177 (1803).

83. *District Board in California*: *United States v. Alvarez*, 567 U.S. 709, 713 (2012).

83. *and a wounded veteran*: Ibid., 714.

83. *wounded many times*: Ibid., 713–14.

84. *save the American flag*: *United States v. Alvarez*, 617 F.3d 1198, 1201 (9th Cir. 2010).

84. *lying was his habit*: *United States v. Alvarez*, 567 U.S. at 713.

84. *Stolen Valor Act of 2005*: Ibid., 714.

84. *Armed Forces of the United States*: Stolen Valor Act of 2005, Pub. L. 109-437, 120 Stat. 3266, 3266.

84. *would put it*: *United States v. Alvarez*, 567 U.S. at 739 (Alito, J., dissenting).

84. *won the Medal of Honor*: Ibid., 741–42 (Alito, J., dissenting).

84. *could not be substantiated*: Ibid., 742 (Alito, J., dissenting).

84. *counterfeits in his courtroom*: Ibid., 742 (Alito, J., dissenting).

85. *dismiss the case against him*: *United States v. Alvarez*, 617 F.3d at 1201.

85. *violated the First Amendment*: *United States v. Alvarez*, 567 U.S. at 714.

85. *his defense counsel*: Although most people know me as a result of my work as a prosecutor for over twenty years, I also served for a decade as a defense lawyer in New York City.

85. *initial trial court level*: United States v. Alvarez, 567 U.S. at 714.
85. *First Amendment grounds*: Ibid.
85. *up to the Supreme Court*: Ibid.
85. *statute going forward*: Ibid., 730 (Breyer, J., concurring in the judgment).
85. *on the books today*: Stolen Valor Act of 2013, Pub. L. 113-12, 127 Stat. 448.
86. *to his conduct*: US Const., Art. I, § 9, cl. 3.
86. *Solicitor General Donald Verrilli Jr.*: Evelyn Douek and Genevieve Lakier, "Rereading *Alvarez*," Knight First Amendment Institute, May 18, 2022, https://knightcolumbia.org/blog/rereading-alvarez.
87. *under the Constitution*: United States v. Alvarez, 567 U.S. at 718.
87. *its actual recipients*: Ibid., 715.
87. *won the medal*: Ibid., 743–44 (Alito, J., dissenting).
87. *any individual recipient*: Ibid., 716.
87. *Six Justices rejected*: Ibid., 715; ibid., 730 (Breyer, J., concurring in the judgment). As Justice Kennedy wrote for the plurality, "The Court has never endorsed the categorical rule the Government advances: that false statements receive no First Amendment protection" (ibid., 719).
87. *with only minor tweaks*: Ibid., 723; ibid., 734 (Breyer, J., concurring in the judgment).
87. *statute as written*: Ibid., 739 (Alito, J., dissenting).
87. *nine of the Justices*: Verrilli later named *Alvarez* as one of the two cases he most regretted losing. See: Douek and Lakier, "Rereading *Alvarez*." Verrilli was joined in his assessment by an unusual bedfellow. Before the Supreme Court ruled, Judge Jay Bybee dissented from the Ninth Circuit's invalidation of the statute: "Public discourse requires that citizens are equally free to praise or to condemn their government and its officials, but I can see no value in false, self-aggrandizing statements by public servants. Indeed, the harm from public officials outright lying to the public on matters of public record should be obvious." See: *United States v. Alvarez*, 617 F.3d at 1233 (Bybee, J., dissenting). Bybee's warning centered on the erosion of truth as a civic value.
88. *claim is counterspeech*: United States v. Alvarez, 567 U.S. at 727.
88. *in a free society*: Ibid.
88. *Supreme Court has blessed*: Ibid., 717.
88. *affronting the First Amendment*: Ibid., 723.
89. *integral to criminal conduct*: Ibid., 717.
89. *not resting on truth*: Ibid., 720.
89. *basis of the legal system*: Ibid., 721.
89. *and countless others*: Ibid., 720.
89. *statements are punishable*: Ibid., 723.
89. *to exacting scrutiny*: Ibid., 724.
90. *to any person*: Ibid., 723.
90. *within a home*: Ibid., 722.
90. *covered mere braggadocio*: Ibid., 723. For support, Kennedy cited the Supreme Court's upholding the prohibition of the false use of the word *Olympic* as exploiting the "commercial magnetism" of the word when used to promote an athletic competition (ibid.).
92. *was the appropriate test*: Ibid., 730 (Breyer, J., concurring in the judgment).

92. *achieve Congress's goals*: Ibid. (Breyer, J., concurring in the judgment). Although American jurists don't like to admit that we apply "proportionality review" (a European concept that involves courts seeming to weigh in on policy decisions, which many believe is inappropriate for the judicial branch to do), that is precisely what the concurrence articulates. It describes its approach as determining whether the harm from the statute is "out of proportion" to its justification.

93. *marketplace of ideas*: Ibid., 732 (Breyer, J., concurring in the judgment).

93. *little First Amendment protection*: Ibid., 732–33 (Breyer, J., concurring in the judgment).

93. *are particularly valueless*: *Hustler Magazine, Inc. v. Falwell*, 485 U.S. 46, 52 (1974).

93. *worthy of constitutional protection*: *Gertz v. Robert Welch, Inc.*, 418 U.S. 323, 340 (1974).

93. *spillover effect*: *United States v. Alvarez*, 567 U.S. at 733 (Breyer, J., concurring in the judgment).

93. *and the like*: Ibid., 731–32 (Breyer, J., concurring in the judgment).

93. *concern such subject matter*: Ibid., 732 (Breyer, J., concurring in the judgment).

93. *its award criteria*: The concurrence engaged in an odd aside, noting that false statements can "preserve a child's innocence" or "provide the sick with comfort" (ibid., 733, Breyer, J., concurring in the judgment). Those examples, while inarguable, are of little practical import to the state's interest in preventing the harms identified in this statute. One can recognize the value of so-called white lies in certain contexts, without giving up the ability to regulate false statements altogether.

94. *weapon to a government*: Ibid., 734 (Breyer, J., concurring in the judgment).

94. *the government disfavors*: Ibid. (Breyer, J., concurring in the judgment).

94. *party in power*: Ibid., 736 (Breyer, J., concurring in the judgment).

94. *pervasiveness of false statements*: Ibid., 734 (Breyer, J., concurring in the judgment).

94. *selectively target minority groups*: Colleen O'Dea, "State police arrest, charge more Black, Hispanic drivers than white," *NJ Spotlight News*, July 9, 2021, https://www.njspotlightnews.org/2021/07/nj-state-police-traffic-stops-more-blacks-more-hispanics-more-summonses-more-arrests/.

95. *Border Czar Tom Homan*: Michael Gold, "Democrats Open Inquiries Into Handling of Homan Investigation," *New York Times*, September 23, 2025, https://www.nytimes.com/2025/09/23/us/politics/tom-homan-democrats-investigation.html. In contrast to the DOJ's treatment of Homan, Trump asked the Justice Department to investigate Jeffrey Epstein's ties to prominent Democrats, and Stephen Miller has taken a central role in the administration's targeting of nonprofits and educational institutions linked to Democrats as "domestic terror networks." See: Melissa Quinn, "Trump asks Justice Department to investigate Epstein's ties to prominent Democrats, banks," *CBS News*, November 15, 2025, https://www.cbsnews.com/news/trump-jeffrey-epstein-justice-department-democrats-banks/; Nandita Bose et al., "Trump's war on the left: Inside the plan to investigate liberal groups," Reuters, October 9, 2025, https://www.reuters.com/legal/government/trumps-war-left-inside-plan-investigate-liberal-groups-2025-10-09/.

95. *weapon of choice*: Devlin Barrett et al., "Grand Jury Indicts Longtime Trump Target, Former F.B.I. Director James Comey," *New York Times*, September 25, 2025, https://www.nytimes.com/2025/09/25/us/politics/james-comey-indicted.html. Two crimes were charged—making a false statement and obstruction of justice.

95. *president Viktor Yanukovych*: Nina Khrushcheva, "Former Ukrainian Prime Minister Yulia Tymoshenko's 'Show Trial,'" *Newsweek*, October 10, 2011, https://www.newsweek.com/former-ukrainian-prime-minister-yulia-tymoshenkos-show-trial-68159.

95. *violated and rarely enforced*: "Ukraine: Tymoshenko on trial in Kiev for abuse of power," *BBC*, June 24, 2011, https://www.bbc.com/news/world-europe-13899740.

96. *in need of reform*: The Court has required a person to show two things to establish selective prosecution. First, she must establish that the government has singled the person out based on a "suspect" criterion, which generally has been defined to mean race, religion, sex, or the assertion of a constitutional right. See: *United States v. Armstrong*, 517 U.S. 456, 465 (1996). Even if that can be shown, she must also prove that the government does not typically prosecute such matters (ibid.). The Court will not give you discovery to prove up these two required elements unless you already have sufficient proof to warrant discovery (ibid., 468). As a practical matter, the Court has largely closed its doors (and eyes) to these claims.

97. *trier of fact*: US Department of Justice, Justice Manual § 9-27.220.

98. *by a unanimous jury*: The grand jury rejected one count and is reported to have voted by 14 (out of a total number of grand jurors of anywhere from 16 to 23) for the other two counts based on the probable cause standard, which means that unless they find more proof, it is hard to see how they would get to proof beyond a reasonable doubt, unanimously, at trial (if the case ever gets that far). See: Eric Tucker and Alanna Durkin Richer, "Lawyers for Comey seek grand jury transcript, bringing fresh challenge to a case pushed by Trump," *WRAL News*, October 30, 2025, https://www.wral.com/news/ap/ace8b-lawyers-for-comey-seek-grand-jury-transcript-bringing-fresh-challenge-to-a-case-pushed-by-trump/.

98. *received this singular award*: *United States v. Alvarez*, 567 U.S. at 709 (Alito, J., dissenting).

98. *watches and designer handbags*: Ibid., 744 (Alito, J., dissenting).

98. *proliferation of knockoffs*: Ibid., 743 (Alito, J., dissenting).

99. *worthy of such protection*: Ibid., 743–44 (Alito, J., dissenting).

99. *caused specific harm*: Ibid., 745 (Alito, J., dissenting).

99. *willing to sustain*: Ibid. (Alito, J., dissenting).

99. *benefit to the prevaricator*: Ibid., 748 (Alito, J., dissenting).

99. *from the deceptive practices*: Ibid. (Alito, J., dissenting).

100. *space for protected speech*: *United States v. Alvarez*, 567 U.S. at 746, 750 (Alito, J., dissenting). Examples of areas for "strategic protection" are defamation and civil fraud actions, where in order to prevent the chilling of truthful speech, the Court has elevated the standard of proof that must be met (ibid., 750–51, Alito, J., dissenting). Such heightened proof requirements will "inevitably" bring some false factual statements within the protection of the First Amendment, but it is justifiable in his view to prevent the chilling of valuable speech.

100. *Alito specifically warns*: Ibid. (Alito, J., dissenting).

100. *suppressing truthful speech*: Ibid. (Alito, J., dissenting).

100. *impossible to ascertain*: Ibid. (Alito, J., dissenting).

100. *arbiter of truth*: Ibid. (Alito, J., dissenting).

100. *may be upheld*: Ibid., 752 (Alito, J., dissenting).

100. *power for political ends*: Ibid. (Alito, J., dissenting).

101. *other tangible benefit*: 18 U.S.C. § 704(b).

101. *obtain certain benefits*: *United States v. Alvarez*, 617 F.3d at 1201 n.2. Because Alvarez had pleaded guilty, there is no full trial record of what the government's evidence would have shown. Of course, the 2013 statute would not be able to be applied retroactively to Alvarez's 2007 conduct anyway because criminal statutes cannot apply retroactively.

101. *including a Purple Heart*: "Canadian Man Sentenced for Stolen Valor and Unlawfully Forging Military Discharge Paperwork," Department of Justice, June 27, 2024, https://www.justice.gov/usao-ndny/pr/canadian-man-sentenced-stolen -valor-and-unlawfully-forging-military-discharge.

101. *plate for his car*: Ibid.

101. *receive a Purple Heart*: Ibid.

101. *and other countries*: "Smith County man sentenced for using stolen valor to defraud investors," Department of Justice, December 8, 2023, https://www.justice.gov/ usao-edtx/pr/smith-county-man-sentenced-using-stolen-valor-defraud-investors.

102. *Distinguished Service Cross*: Ibid.

102. *to woo investors*: Ibid.

102. *eleven years in jail*: Ibid.

Chapter 5

106. *countries' constitutional rights*: Ruth Bader Ginsburg, foreword to *The Constitutional Jurisprudence of the Federal Republic of Germany* (Durham, NC: Duke University Press, 2012), xi.

107. *president Jair Bolsonaro*: Andrea Mitchell and Julie Cerullo, "Trump hits Brazil-ian products with 50% tariffs over Bolsonaro," *NBC News*, August 2, 2025, https: //www.nbcnews.com/politics/trump-administration/trump-brazilian-products -tariffs-bolsonaro-rcna222534.

107. *nationalism and social conservatism*: "'Not worthy of rape' deputy says she fears for Brazil under a President Bolsonaro," *France24* (Agence France-Presse), October 19, 2018, https://www.france24.com/en/20181019-not-worthy-rape-deputy-says -she-fears-brazil-under-president-bolsonaro; "Jair Bolsonaro Fast Facts," *CNN*, September 17, 2025, https://www.cnn.com/world/americas/jair-bolsonaro-fast -facts.

107. *not my type*: Ibid. Trump made similar comments about E. Jean Carroll. See: "Trump: Woman who accused him of sexual assault not his type," *AP News*, June 24, 2019, https://apnews.com/article/62111c338d9a4862ae621419877d7f14.

107. *innocents will die*: Sean Purdy, "Here's What Jair Bolsonaro Thinks," *Jacobin*, October 28, 2018, https://jacobin.com/2018/10/jair-bolsonaro-quotes-brazil-election.

107. *let's do the coup*: Lucia Binding, "'Trump of the Tropics' — Controversial quotes by Brazil's new president Jair Bolsonaro," *Sky News*, January 1, 2019, https: //news.sky.com/story/trump-of-the-tropics-controversial-quotes-by-brazils -new-president-jair-bolsonaro-11539063.

107. *lead in the polls*: Flora Charner and Marcia Reverdosa, "Far-right candidate Jair Bolsonaro wins presidential election in Brazil," *CNN*, October 29, 2018, https: //www.cnn.com/2018/10/28/americas/brazil-election.

107. *in October 2018*: Ibid.

107. *Brazilian electoral system*: "Brazil: Bolsonaro Threatens Democratic Rule," Human Rights Watch, September 15, 2021, https://www.hrw.org/news/2021/09/15/brazil-bolsonaro-threatens-democratic-rule.

108. *reelection and lost*: Jack Nicas, "Brazil Ejects Bolsonaro and Brings Back Leftist Former Leader Lula," *New York Times*, October 30, 2022, https://www.nytimes.com/2022/10/30/world/americas/lula-election-results-brazil-bolsonaro.html.

108. *the National Congress*: Chris Cameron, "The attack on Brazil's seat of government resembles the storming of the U.S. Capitol on Jan. 6, 2021," *New York Times*, January 8, 2023, https://www.nytimes.com/2023/01/08/world/americas/brazil-jan-6-riots.html.

108. *numerous police officers*: Ibid.

108. *Bolsonaro's wrongful defeat*: Ibid.

108. *double-digit jail sentences*: Diane Jeantet and Diarlei Rodrigues, "Brazil observes anniversary of the anti-democratic uprising in the capital," *AP News*, January 8, 2024, https://apnews.com/article/brazil-riots-anniversary-bolsonaro-lula-41c7e872916ca88ffdb8c27409726dd9; "Brazil sentences three to over 14 years for storming government buildings," Reuters, September 14, 2023, https://www.reuters.com/world/americas/brazils-supreme-court-convicts-first-defendant-january-8th-trial-2023-09-14/.

108. *women they vilified*: Erica Orden, "Trump loses bid to overturn \$83.3M E. Jean Carroll defamation judgment," *Politico*, September 8, 2025, https://www.politico.com/news/2025/09/08/trump-e-jean-carroll-appeal-ruling-00550333; Camilo Rocha and Daniela Gonzalez-Roman, "Brazilian court orders Bolsonaro to compensate journalist for sexist remarks," *CNN*, June 29, 2022, https://www.cnn.com/2022/06/29/americas/bolsonaro-court-order-compensation-sexist-remarks-intl-latam.

108. *or political party*: Lei Complementar No. 64, de 18 de Maio de 1965, art. 22 (Brazil).

109. *interest of electoral integrity*: Ibid., art. 23. For this and other citations to Brazil authorities, we have used translations from the original Portugese.

109. *for a set period of time*: Ibid., art. 1, I; ibid., art. 22, XIV.

109. *Clean Slate Law*: Lei Complementar No. 135, de 4 de Junho de 2010, art. 2 (Brazil).

109. *petitions seeking election reform*: Rachel Glickhouse and Luisa Leme, "Explainer: Brazil's Clean Record Law," Americas Society and Council of the Americas, August 26, 2014, https://www.as-coa.org/articles/explainer-brazils-clean-record-law.

109. *mandatory disqualification period*: Lei Complementar No. 64 art. 1, I; ibid., art. 22, XIV.

109. *the following [eight] years*: Ibid., art. 1, I.

110. *dangers of disinformation*: To put this ruling in context, it is worth noting some similarities and difference between the Brazilian constitution's free speech protections and our own. Our Constitution has a simple, short statement, leaving much room for the courts to interpret its contours and for what to do when the First Amendment rubs up against other constitutional rights.

Brazil has strong protections as well, but they are more specific and detailed. Article 5 of the Brazilian constitution provides:

IV — "Freedom of expression is guaranteed, anonymity being prohibited."

IX — "Freedom of expression of intellectual, artistic, scientific and communicative activity is guaranteed, regardless of censorship or licensing."

XIV — "Everyone is guaranteed access to information and the confidentiality of sources is protected when necessary for the exercise of a profession."

In practice, Brazil permits restrictions on so-called hate speech, including racist speech, as violative of human dignity and equality, which are also protected rights in its constitution (Constituição Federal art. 5, XLII — Brazil). We, on the other hand, do not restrict hate speech unless it is a true threat or an exhortation to imminent violence. Our Supreme Court has held that speech that demeans on the basis of race, ethnicity, gender, religion, age, disability, or any other similar ground "is hateful; but the proudest boast of our free speech jurisprudence is that we protect the freedom to express 'the thought that we hate.'" See: *Matal v. Tam*, 582 U.S. 218, 246 (2017).

110. *seeing Bolsonaro charged*: Jack Nicas, "Brazil Bars Bolsonaro From Office for Election-Fraud Claims," *New York Times*, June 30, 2023, https://www.nytimes .com/2023/06/30/world/americas/bolsonaro-brazil-banned-office.html.

110. *and found liable*: Ibid.

110. *article 22 of Complementary Law no. 64*: T.S.E.J., Ação de Investigação Judicial Eleitoral No. 0600814-85.2022.6.00.0000, Relator: Min. Benedito Gonçalves, 07.04.23, 3 (Brazil).

110. *statements were not merely false*: Ibid., 112.

110. *infected by fraud*: Ibid., 146.

111. *compromised by fraud*: Ibid., 370.

111. *company's voting machines*: Ibid.

111. *to the contrary*: Ibid., 190–94.

111. *about election tampering*: Ibid., 437–40.

111. *inflame his supporters*: Ibid.

111. *found Bolsonaro liable*: Nicas, "Brazil Bars Bolsonaro."

111. *the Brazilian statutes*: Ação de Investigação Judicial Eleitoral No. 0600814 -85.2022.6.00.0000, at 439.

112. *and the electorate*: Ibid., 448.

112. *lies had fomented*: Ibid., 439.

112. *through October 2030*: Ibid., 435. The court used the election date of October 2, 2022, as the starting point for the ban. This means that Bolsonaro is legally barred from holding office until October 2030 (ibid.).

112. *that highest office*: Following the TSE's ruling, Bolsonaro's legal team promptly filed an appeal with Brazil's Supreme Federal Court (the Supremo Tribunal Federal or STF), the nation's highest court charged with constitutional review. See: Recurso Extraordinário com Agravo 1474354, Supremo Tribunal Federal, https://portal.stf.jus.br/processos/detalhe.asp. The appeal challenges the constitutionality of criminalizing false speech about elections under the free-speech protections in Brazil's Constitution. See: Recurso Extraordinário,

S.T.F.J. Ação de Investigação Judicial Eleitoral No. 0600814-85.2022.6.00.0000, Relator: Min. Luiz Fux, 06.10.23, (Brazil), 9, https://static.poder360.com.br/2023 /10/recurso-inelegibilidade-jair-bolsonaro-tse-6-out-2023.pdf. The defense also attacks the eight-year ineligibility penalty as an excessive restriction on political rights and participation (ibid., 11).

113. *that separate offense*: Ana Ionova and Jack Nicas, "Bolsonaro Sentenced to 27 Years in Prison for Plotting Coup in Brazil," *New York Times*, September 11, 2025, https://www.nytimes.com/2025/09/11/world/americas/bolsonaro-convicted -coup-attempt.html.

113. *went to trial*: Ibid.

113. *and the lead judge*: Ana Ionova and Jack Nicas, "Trump Escalates Fight With Brazil, Taking Aim at Its Economy and Politics," *New York Times*, July 30, 2025, https://www.nytimes.com/2025/07/30/world/americas/trump-sanctions-brazil -judge-bolsonaro.html.

113. *against the judges*: Ibid.

113. *treatment of Bolsonaro*: Ibid.

113. *and international disgrace*: Natalie Sherman and Nadine Yousif, "Trump threatens Brazil with 50% tariff and demands Bolsonaro's trial end," *BBC*, July 9, 2025, https://www.bbc.com/news/articles/c784ee81y4zo.

113. *to convict Bolsonaro*: Ionova and Nicas, "Bolsonaro Sentenced."

113. *three months in jail*: Ibid. Brazil also separately criminalizes certain political lies, although Bolsonaro was not charged with that offense. It is a criminal offense under Article 323 of the Electoral Code if a person intentionally lies about a candidate. It is a crime to "disseminate, in electoral propaganda or during the electoral campaign period, facts that one knows to be false concerning political parties or candidates and which are capable of influencing the electorate. See: Lei Complementar No. 64 art. 323. That crime is punishable for up to year (ibid.).

113. *bad for Brazil*: Ricardo Brito et al., "Brazil's Bolsonaro sentenced to 27 years after landmark coup plot conviction," Reuters, September 12, 2025, https://www .reuters.com/world/americas/brazils-bolsonaro-sentenced-27-years-after -landmark-coup-plot-conviction-2025-09-12/.

113. *above the law*: Sherman and Yousif, "Trump Threatens Brazil."

113. *don't want an emperor*: Ibid.

114. *certain election lies*: R (Woolas) v. Speaker of the House of Commons [2010] EWHC 3169, [2012] QB 1 [9] (Eng.).

114. *in fact believe it*: Ibid.

114. *Representation of the People Act*: Ibid.

114. *falsely accusing his opponent*: Adam Wagner, "Analysis: Woolas loses election court challenge, court clarifies constitutional role," *UK Human Rights Blog*, December 3, 2010, https://ukhumanrightsblog.com/2010/12/03/analysis-woolas -loses-election-court-challenge-supreme-court-next/; "Lying Labour MP Phil Woolas stripped of seat in election in race row," *The Standard*, April 12, 2012, https://www.standard.co.uk/hp/front/lying-labour-mp-phil-woolas-stripped -of-seat-in-election-in-race-row-6532989.html.

NOTES

115. *stripped of his election*: "Lying Labor MP," *The Standard*. The law was unsuccessfully invoked in 2015, when a court found that although a candidate told a "blatant lie" it was not proven beyond a reasonable doubt that the lie was designed to mislead voters about the challenger's personal conduct. See: Severin Carrell, "Alistair Carmichael: Election Court Rejects Attempt to Unseat MP," *The Guardian*, December 9, 2015, https://www.theguardian.com/uk-news/2015/dec/09/alistair-carmichael-lib-dem-election-court-throws-out-attempt-to-unseat-mp.

115. *for five years*: Joseph Ataman et al., "Far-right leader Marine Le Pen banned from 2027 presidential race, throwing French politics into disarray," *CNN*, March 31, 2025, https://edition.cnn.com/2025/03/31/europe/marine-le-pen-embezzlement-trial-verdict-france-intl.

115. *up to ten years*: Code Pénal art. 131-26-1 (France).

115. *crimes for disqualification*: Ataman et al., "Marine Le Pen Banned"; Code Pénal art. 432-15, 432-17.

115. *remains in effect*: Victor Goury-Laffont, "Le Pen asks European Court of Human Rights to help her quash election ban," *Politico*, July 8, 2025, https://www.politico.eu/article/marine-le-pen-european-court-of-human-rights-election-ban/.

116. *abstain from voting*: Code Électoral art. L97.

116. *host of serious offenses*: Juliette Jabkhiro et al., "Former French President Sarkozy handed 5-year jail term in stunning downfall," Reuters, September 25, 2025, https://www.reuters.com/world/europe/french-court-deliver-verdict-sarkozy-corruption-trial-2025-09-25/.

117. *State of New York*: Ben Protess et al., "Trump Convicted on All Counts to Become America's First Felon President," *New York Times*, May 30, 2024, https://www.nytimes.com/2024/05/30/nyregion/trump-convicted-hush-money-trial.html.

117. *in our country*: "Restoration of Rights Project," Collateral Consequences Resource Center, https://ccresourcecenter.org/restoration-2-2/.

117. *the 2016 election*: Protess et al., "Trump Convicted."

117. *stories about himself*: Ibid.

117. *conviction of a crime*: "Restoration of Rights Project," Collateral Consequences Resource Center.

117. *office in that state*: Ibid.

117. *holding federal office*: *Trump v. Anderson*, 601 U.S. 100, 111 (2024).

118. *to the enemies thereof*: US Const. art. XIV, § 3.

118. *for president again*: *Trump v. Anderson*, 601 U.S. at 106.

119. *certify the election results*: Ibid.

119. *to retain power*: Ibid., 107.

119. *no person shall*: Ibid.

119. *fomented an insurrection*: Ibid.

119. *second impeachment process*: Domenico Montanaro, "Senate Acquits Trump In Impeachment Trial — Again," *NPR*, February 13, 2021, https://www.npr.org/sections/trump-impeachment-trial-live-updates/2021/02/13/967098840/senate-acquits-trump-in-impeachment-trial-again.

119. *about election fraud*: Lisa Mascaro et al., "Trump impeached after Capitol riot in historic second charge," *AP News*, January 13, 2021, https://apnews.com/article/trump-impeachment-vote-capitol-siege-0a6f2a348a6e43f27d5e1dc486027860.

119. *including seven Republicans*: Montanaro, "Senate Acquits Trump."

119. *The case went up*: *Trump v. Anderson*, 601 U.S. at 117.

120. *states actually do*: Ibid., 111; "Restoration of Rights Project," Collateral Consequences Resource Center.

120. *in the fifty states*: *Trump v. Anderson*, 601 U.S. at 116.

120. *officeholders and candidates*: Ibid., 111. More controversial was the language that the federal government could only enforce federal restrictions through acts of Congress, not the courts (ibid., 117). Three Justices dissented from that part of the decision, with Justice Barrett separately writing to note that the majority's reaching this issue was unfortunate, given that it was unnecessary and marred an otherwise unanimous resolution of the case (ibid., 117–18, Barrett, J., concurring in part and concurring in the judgment; ibid., 118, Sotomayor, J., concurring in the judgment).

120. *find it improper*: Ibid., 109.

120. *The Court also observed*: Ibid., 111, 114.

120. *new constitutional amendment*: Ibid., 114.

121. *passed a criminal statute*: Ibid., 114–15.

121. *on the books*: Ibid.

121. *under the United States*: 18 U.S.C. § 2383 (emphasis added).

121. *due to disuse*: Act of June 25, 1948, ch. 646, § 39, 62 Stat. 869, 993.

122. *office would qualify*: Jack Smith, Special Counsel, *Final Report on the Special Counsel's Investigations and Prosecutions* (2025), 62, 64, https://www.justice.gov /storage/Report-of-Special-Counsel-Smith-Volume-1-January-2025.pdf.

122. *and controversial territory*: Ibid., 66–67; Jack Smith, "The State of the United States: A Conversation with Jack Smith," moderated by Andrew Weissmann, October 14, 2025, by University College London Faculty of Laws, YouTube, 1:01:55, https://www.youtube.com/watch?v=DR79GW6SvxE.

122. *running for office*: Brazil has two variations on this French model. It does not require a criminal conviction to be subject to debarment (thus it is similar to Congress's Enforcement Act of 1870, which only required a civil finding against the person). See: Lei Complementar No. 64 art. 1, I; ibid., art. 22, XIV; *Trump v. Anderson*, 601 U.S. at 114. Brazil also limits its disqualification to those found to have engaged in intentional election and political abuse, not the panoply of offenses that carry this penalty in France. See: Ação de Investigação Judicial Eleitoral No. 0600814-85.2022.6.00.0000, at 112.

122. *existence of the Holocaust*: Strafgesetzbuch [StGB], § 130(3) (Germany).

122. *done this as well*: Michael J. Bazyler, "Holocaust Denial Laws and Other Legislation Criminalizing Promotion of Nazism," *Genocide Prevention Now* (2009): 2–8, https://bcsh.bard.edu/files/2019/06/Holocaust-denial-laws.pdf.

123. *freedom of speech*: Dieter Grimm, "The Holocaust Denial Decision of the Federal Constitutional Court of Germany," in *Extreme Speech and Democracy*, ed. Ivan Hare and James Weinstein (Oxford, UK: Oxford University Press, 2009), 557–61.

123. *stirred-up majorities*: Ginsburg, foreword to *Constitutional Jurisprudence*, xi.

123. *five years or a fine*: For the full text, see: StGB, § 130(3). Holocaust denial is generally understood in European Union law as the questioning of "the state-sponsored, systematic persecution and mass murder of Jews, whom the Nazi

regime and its collaborators sought to annihilate along with other persecuted groups, such as Roma and Sinti." See: Piotr Bąkowski, "Holocaust Denial in Criminal Law: Legal Framework in Selected EU Member States," *European Parliamentary Research Service*, (2022): 1, https://www.europarl.europa.eu /RegData/etudes/BRIE/2021/698043/EPRS_BRI%282021%29698043_EN.pdf.

124. *military medal recipient*: United States v. Alvarez, 567 U.S. 709, 722 (2012).

124. *by the law*: StGB, § 130(3).

124. *the public peace*: Ibid.

124. *other tangible benefit*: Stolen Valor Act of 2013, Pub. L. 113-12, 127 Stat. 448.

125. *amend the statute*: The German Holocaust denial law presents a host of legal questions, including: What is the scope of the vague term *downplay*? What is the scope of the term *assembly*—is it more than two people, and if so, how many constitutes an "assembly?" What constitutes disturbing the "peace?" How likely does it have to be that there will be such a disturbance? Is there an intent standard for a false statement of fact, as we would have in the United States? And who bears the burden of establishing the case, and what level of proof must be met to prove the case (i.e., is it a "preponderance of the evidence" or is it higher, given the potential stakes at issue)? The answers to the questions are far beyond the scope of this book.

125. *upcoming gathering in Munich*: Bundesverfassungsgericht [BVerfG], April 13, 1994, 90 Entscheidungen des Bundesverfassungsgerichts [BVerfGE] 241 (Germany); Grimm, "The Holocaust Denial Decision," 558.

126. *Third Reich never happened*: R. J. van Pelt, *The Case for Auschwitz* (Bloomington, IN: Indiana University Press, 2002), 48.

126. *refer to Holocaust denial*: Grimm, "The Holocaust Denial Decision," 558.

126. *heard the case*: BVerfG, 90 BVerfGE 241, para. 18.

126. *opinions from facts*: Ibid., para. 26–27.

126. *true or false*: Ibid., para. 26.

126. *formation of opinion*: Ibid., para. 27.

126. *dangerous or harmless*: Ibid., para. 26.

126. *the court wrote*: Ibid., para. 27.

126. *worthy of protection*: Ibid., para. 28.

127. *could be difficult*: Ibid., para. 29.

127. *protect the statement*: Ibid., para. 29.

127. *representations of fact*: Ibid., para. 34. The court was nuanced in thinking about the separation of opinion and fact, and as opinions are "usually based on assumptions about facts," the court was willing to accord these facts some protection (ibid., para. 27). Statements of fact are protected under freedom of expression "to the extent they are the foundation for opinions" (ibid., para. 27). But where the so-called fact contributes nothing to the formation of opinion, there is no protection (ibid., para. 28).

127. *entitled to protection*: United States v. Alvarez, 567 U.S. at 723; ibid., 733 (Breyer, J., concurring in the judgment); ibid., 739 (Alito, J., dissenting).

127. *freedom of expression*: BVerfG, 90 BVerfGE 241, para. 31.

128. *before the law*: Grundgesetz [GG] art. 3, translation at http://www.gesetze-im -internet.de/englisch_gg/index.html.

128. *religious liberty*: Ibid., art. 4.

128. *assembly and association*: Ibid., art. 8.

128. *human dignity*: Ibid., art. 1.

128. *one's personality*: Ibid., art. 2.

128. *rights to education*: Ibid., art. 7.

128. *to occupation*: Ibid., art. 9.

128. *posts and telecommunications*: Ibid., art. 10.

128. *and historical analysis*: BVerfG, 90 BVerfGE 241, para. 34.

129. *meeting was prohibited*: It is worth reminding younger readers that, commencing in 1946, shortly after World War II, the Allies afforded numerous Nazi defendants full trials in Nuremburg, Germany, to determine their individual liability. See: United States Holocaust Memorial Museum, "Combating Holocaust Denial: Evidence of the Holocaust presented at Nuremberg," *Holocaust Encyclopedia*, https://encyclopedia.ushmm.org/content/en/article/combating-holocaust -denial-evidence-of-the-holocaust-presented-at-nuremberg. Those trials established incontrovertible proof of the Holocaust through, among other things, voluminous documentary evidence, including the defendants' own statements and the Nazi regime's contemporaneous meticulous records. As a result of such evidence, the factual defenses put forth in the Nuremberg trials hinged not on claims that the Holocaust did not occur, but rather on a denial of personal awareness or culpability for it. See: United States Holocaust Memorial Museum, "Nuremberg Trials," *Holocaust Encyclopedia*, https://encyclopedia.ushmm.org /content/en/article/the-nuremberg-trials.

129. *under the German constitution*: BVerfG, 90 BVerfGE 241, para. 43.

130. *against him or her*: Ibid. The German ruling is in keeping with that of other European countries and the European Court of Human Rights (the ECtHR). The latter has confronted repeatedly the legality of laws banning Holocaust denial. See: Bąkowski, "Holocaust Denial." In examining the statutes, the court took a similar path to that of Germany and, in part, the United States in the *Alvarez* case. The ECtHR distinguishes speech about a clearly established fact, on the one hand, and opinion or facts still validly debated (ibid.). If the false speech is about a proven fact, the court then balances free speech against other protected rights (ibid.).

In assessing the states' interests, the ECtHR found Holocaust denial particularly dangerous, given its history (ibid.). It appreciated the state's interest in banning such denial "especially in States which have experienced the Nazi horrors, and which may be regarded as having a special moral responsibility to distance themselves from the mass atrocities that they have perpetrated or abetted" (ibid.). The ECtHR found that Holocaust denial has been "presumed... to incite to hatred or intolerance, a presumption that allows for such incitement not to be proved in each case" (ibid.).

130. *ever to be undone*: *Brown v. Bd. of Educ.*, 347 U.S. 483, 494 (1954). The German court's recognition of other constitutional rights and balancing of various rights is reminiscent of the approach of Justice Breyer in *Alvarez*. See: *United States v. Alvarez*, 567 U.S., 730 (Breyer, J., concurring in the judgment). Balancing tests can lead to disparate results, given that judges may weigh differently the interests

at stake. In Germany, prohibitions on hate speech have passed muster under its constitution. See: StGB, § 130(1). The same is not true in the United States, where prohibitions of hate speech have been found to be inconsistent with the First Amendment. See: *Snyder v. Phelps*, 562 U.S. 443, 448, 461 (2011). See also endnote, *dangers of disinformation* (203–204).

131. *for as well*: Lei Complementar No. 64 art. 1, I; Representation of the People Act (1983) c. 2, § 106 (Eng.).

131. *involving false speech*: Loi 2016-1691 art. 19.

131. *could affect public safety*: StGB § 130(3).

132. *to do the same*: Amy O'Kruk and Curt Merrill, "Donald Trump's criminal cases, in one place," *CNN*, January 10, 2025, https://www.cnn.com/interactive/2023/07/politics/trump-indictments-criminal-cases/.

132. *A new Congress*: Politicians at the federal or state level who are beholden to Trump or Trumpism are surely not going to take on these or any other reforms that could hold political lies to account. But federal and state politicians not so aligned, of either party, could seek to implement needed reforms.

132. *who can use them*: *Youngstown Sheet & Tube Co. v. Sawyer*, 343 U.S. 579, 654 (1952) (Jackson, J., concurring in the judgment and opinion).

Chapter 6

136. *for a false filing*: The FEC already warns candidates about the ramifications of lying to it about financial material they must submit. Section 1001 of Title 18 of the United States Code makes knowing, intentional, and material false statements a crime. The proposed new law could include a right for the candidate to challenge in an expedited proceeding in court any FEC action to withhold funds based on a determination of falsehood, and a heightened standard of proof that the agency would have to meet to establish falsehood. The law could also specify how often the certifications must be made (e.g., every thirty days).

138. *course to chart*: Scott Bomboy, "How a college term paper led to a constitutional amendment," National Constitution Center, May 7, 2024, https://constitutioncenter.org/blog/how-a-c-grade-college-term-paper-led-to-a-constitutional-amendment.

138. *constitutional ratification*: Alex Cohen and Wilfred U. Codrington III, "The Equal Rights Amendment Explained," Brennan Center for Justice, January 23, 2020, https://www.brennancenter.org/our-work/research-reports/equal-rights-amendment-explained.

138. *prohibit his speech*: Lei Complementar No. 64, de Maio de 18 de 1990, art. 1, I (Brazil).

139. *run for president*: US Const., art. II, § 1, cl. 5.

139. *be on a ballot*: Charles McCarthy, *The Wisconsin Idea* (New York: Macmillan, 1912), 88–89; H. Feldman, "The Direct Primary in New York State," *American Political Science Review* 11, no. 3 (1917): 494, https://doi.org/10.2307/1944250; Alan Ware, *The American Direct Primary: Party Institutionalization and Transformation in the North* (Cambridge, UK: Cambridge University Press, 2002), 112, 221 n.25.

139. *running for public office*: Gary Fields and Josh Funk, "State laws vary widely on whether felons can run for office," *AP News*, January 19, 2023, https://apnews.com/article/illinois-state-government-west-virginia-new-mexico-nebraska-legal-proceedings-a640fea829456d6cfb2c0d9e97a1dfa3.

140. *judge or jury*: *Baxter v. Palmigiano*, 425 U.S. 308, 318 (1976); *Griffin v. California*, 380 U.S. 609, 614 (1965).

140. *and even murderers*: Zolan Kanno-Youngs and Luke Broadwater, "Trump Gives Clemency to More Than Two Dozen, Including Political Allies," *New York Times*, May 30, 2025, https://www.nytimes.com/2025/05/28/us/politics/trump-pardons-hoover-grimm-chrisley.html; Tom Dreisbach, "Criminal records of Jan. 6 rioters pardoned by Trump include rape, domestic violence," *NPR*, January 30, 2025, https://www.npr.org/2025/01/30/nx-s1-5276336/donald-trump-jan-6-rape-assault-pardons-rioters; William K. Rashbaum et al., "Former President of Honduras Is Freed From Prison After Trump Pardon," *New York Times*, December 2, 2025, https://www.nytimes.com/2025/12/02/us/politics/hernandez-honduras-trump.html.

140. *only to criminal matters*: Richard Lempert, "Presidential pardons: Settled law, unsettled issues, and a downside for Trump," Brookings Institute, January 17, 2021, https://www.brookings.edu/articles/presidential-pardons-settled-law-unsettled-issues-and-a-downside-for-trump/.

140. *federal matching funds*: "Establishing eligibility to receive presidential primary matching fund payments," Federal Election Commission, https://www.fec.gov/help-candidates-and-committees/understanding-public-funding-presidential-elections/establishing-eligibility-presidential-primary-matching-funds/.

140. *file accurate reports*: 11 C.F.R. § 104.3. 18 U.S.C. § 1001.

141. *damage to a democracy*: Lei Complementar No. 64 art. 1, I.

141. *Supreme Court's* Alvarez *decision*: *United States v. Alvarez*, 567 U.S. 709 (2012).

142. *protected free speech*: Ibid., 734 (Breyer, J., concurring in the judgment).

142. *to make it constitutional*: Stolen Valor Act of 2013, Pub. L. 113-12, 127 Stat. 448.

142. *process and results*: *United States v. Alvarez*, 567 U.S. at 743 (Alito, J., dissenting).

142. *no functioning democracy*: The third hypothetical US law imports the first US model, so it shares this same restricted application to only a subset of political lies.

144. *make it constitutional*: Ibid., 723.

144. *a chilling effect on truthful speech*: Ibid., 723; ibid., 733 (Breyer, J., concurring in the judgment); ibid., 739 (Alito, J., dissenting).

145. *insurrection and rebellion*: US Const. amend. XIV, § 3.

146. *and the like*: *United States v. Alvarez*, 567 U.S., 749.

146. *no objective truth*: Ibid., 740 (Alito, J., dissenting).

146. *banning Holocaust denial*: Strafgesetzbuch [StGB], § 130(3).

147. *new legal framework*: *Trump v. United States*, 603 U.S. 593, 606 (2024).

147. *Supreme Court's 2024 decision*: Ibid.

148. *losing the 2020 election*: Ibid., 602.

148. *all the charges*: Ibid., 604.

148. *the president exclusively*: Ibid., 607.

148. *one such power*: Ibid., 608.

148. *through a federal statute*: Ibid.

148. *If, for example*: The import of the Supreme Court's extraordinary decision is that it may be extended to those in government who carry out the president's orders. See: Trevor W. Morrison, "All The President's Men," *New York University Law Review Online*, August 20, 2025, 27–33, https://nyulawreview.org/case-comments/all -the-presidents-men/.

148. *in an official capacity*: Ibid., 629.

149. *after the person was president*: Ibid., 639.

149. *candidate seeking reelection*: Ibid., 629.

149. *win the 2016 election*: Ben Protess et al., "Trump Convicted on All Counts to Become America's First Felon President," *New York Times*, May 30, 2024, https: //www.nytimes.com/2024/05/30/nyregion/trump-convicted-hush-money-trial .html.

149. *fall into this bucket*: Trump is appealing this determination, along with the entire case.

As Justice Amy Coney Barrett observed, differentiating when a president is acting in an unofficial capacity as opposed to an official one can be difficult at times. Justice Barrett dissented from the part of the majority decision that sent back to the district court the issue of whether Trump's alleged conduct with respect to establishing slates of fake "alternative" electors was within his presidential functions. "Sorting private from official conduct sometimes will be difficult—but not always. Take the President's alleged attempt to organize alternative slates of electors…In my view, that conduct is private and therefore not entitled to protection…I see no plausible argument for barring prosecution of that alleged conduct." See: *Trump v. United States*, 603 U.S. at 653 n.2. Barrett noted that the president simply has no official role in this area, so a president is not functioning as both judge and jury of his own election (ibid.).

149. *the president exclusively*: *Trump v. United States*, 603 U.S. at 609.

149. *his presidential authority*: Ibid., 614–15. I have written with Mary McCord, my *Main Justice* podcast co-host, about the ahistorical nature of the Court's reasoning and its unleashing of precisely the tit-for-tat cycle of factionalism that it claimed to be seeking to thwart. See: Mary McCord and Andrew Weissmann, "How the Supreme Court Paved the Way for Revenge Prosecutions," *New York Times*, November 1, 2025, https://www.nytimes.com/2025/11/01/opinion/comey -james-trump-immunity.html.

149. *framework it set out*: Ibid., 624–25.

150. *that factual issue*: Ibid., 653 n.2 (Barrett, J., concurring in part).

150. *to a civil law*: Although the Supreme Court in its *Trump* presidential criminal immunity decision broke much new ground, the Court had previously afforded a president absolute civil immunity from damage actions in connection with official presidential actions. See: *Nixon v. Fitzgerald*, 457 U.S. 731, 755–56 (1982). That does not extend to non-presidential actions, as the Court decided in ruling that President Clinton could be sued civilly for alleged sexual harassment. See: *Clinton v. Jones*, 520 U.S. 681, 705 (1997).

Chapter 7

154. *presidential rival Joe Biden*: "Trump impeachment: How Ukraine story unfolded," *BBC*, December 19, 2019, https://www.bbc.com/news/world-us-canada -50323605.

154. *against political adversaries*: Jonathan Yerushalmy, "How the National Enquirer boosted Trump and smeared his opponents: 'The only choice for president,'" *The Guardian*, April 24, 2024, https://www.theguardian.com/us-news/2024/apr/24 /trump-national-enquirer; Ximeno Bustillo, "The last words: What each side said in closing arguments for Trump's New York trial," *NPR*, May 28, 2024, https: //www.npr.org/2024/05/28/nx-s1-4984121/trump-trial-closing-arguments-jury -new-york; "D.A. Bragg Announces 34-Count Felony Trial Conviction of Donald J. Trump," Manhattan District Attorney, May 30, 2024, https://manhattanda .org/d-a-bragg-announces-34-count-felony-trial-conviction-of-donald-j-trump/.

154. *The jury later went on*: Ben Protess et al., "Trump Convicted on All Counts to Become America's First Felon President," *New York Times*, May 30, 2024, https: //www.nytimes.com/2024/05/30/nyregion/trump-convicted-hush-money-trial .html.

155. *the January 6 insurrection*: Bill Chappell, "House Impeaches Trump A 2nd Time, Citing Insurrection At U.S. Capitol," *NPR*, January 13, 2021, https://www.npr .org/sections/trump-impeachment-effort-live-updates/2021/01/13/956449072 /house-impeaches-trump-a-2nd-time-citing-insurrection-at-u-s-capitol.

155. *of the electoral votes*: Domenico Montanaro, "Senate Acquits Trump In Impeach-ment Trial — Again," *NPR*, February 13, 2021, https://www.npr.org/sections /trump-impeachment-trial-live-updates/2021/02/13/967098840/senate-acquits -trump-in-impeachment-trial-again.

155. *may get it wrong*: The work of the Innocence Project is built on this systemic problem, even in criminal cases in which we use the highest standard of proof we have in the law — beyond a reasonable doubt — in order to reduce the risk of error. That legal standard lowers the risk of error; it does not eliminate it. I had the privilege of partnering with the Innocence Project when I was the general counsel of the FBI. We instigated a top-to-bottom review of the FBI Laboratory's use of hair-comparison data in thousands of criminal trials across the nation. See: "FBI Testimony on Microscopic Hair Analysis Contained Errors in at Least 90 Percent of Cases in Ongoing Review," Federal Bureau of Investigation, April 20, 2015, https://www.fbi.gov/news/press-releases/fbi-testimony-on-microscopic-hair -analysis-contained-errors-in-at-least-90-percent-of-cases-in-ongoing-review.

156. *in the 2020 election*: "Results of Lawsuits Regarding the 2020 Elections," Cam-paign Legal Center, https://campaignlegal.org/results-lawsuits-regarding-2020 -elections. Some of Trump's lawyers even backtracked in court to say that they were not alleging material fraud in the election. See: Tessa Berenson Rogers, "Donald Trump And His Lawyers Are Making Sweeping Allegations of Voter Fraud In Public. In Court, They Say No Such Thing," *Time*, November 20, 2020, https://time.com/5914377/donald-trump-no-evidence-fraud/.

157. *financial and media sources*: See Chapter 3 on the role of the current media landscape in eroding the marketplace of ideas. Also, see: Norman J. Ornstein,

"Will Our Corporate Media Godzillas Have the Guts to Defend Democracy?," *New Republic*, September 30, 2025, https://newrepublic.com/article/201041 /corporate-media-consolidation-defend-democracy-trump; Giuliano da Empoli, *L'heure des Predateurs* (London: Pushkin Press, 2025).

158. *two-year federal position*: Congress could make any of these new laws applicable to *appointed* federal officials who lie, of course, not just to elected federal officials.

159. *this dual goal in action*: Carrie Kahn, "A Brazil court has banned Bolsonaro from running for election until 2030," *NPR*, June 30, 2023, https://www.npr.org/2023/06 /30/1185364211/brazil-bolsonaro-court-banned-election.

159. *sustain a civil case*: *Tellabs, Inc. v. Makor Issues & Rts., Ltd.*, 551 U.S. 308, 324 (2007).

159. *support their claims*: *Bell Atlantic Corp. v. Twombly*, 550 U.S. 544, 555–56 (2007).

159. *case is dismissed outright*: Ibid.

160. *the law to be*: The Twenty-Second Amendment to the Constitution provides in Section 1: "No person shall be elected to the office of the President more than twice, and no person who has held the office of President, or acted as President, for more than two years of a term to which some other person was elected President shall be elected to the office of the President more than once."

160. *after being president*: Margaret A. Hogan, "John Quincy Adams: Life after the Presidency," University of Virginia Miller Center, https://millercenter.org /president/jqadams/life-after-the-presidency; Elizabeth R. Varon, "Andrew Johnson: Life after the Presidency," University of Virginia Miller Center, https: //millercenter.org/president/johnson/life-after-the-presidency.

161. *there has been talk*: Kristen Welker and Megan Lebowitz, "Trump won't rule out seeking a third term in the White House, tells NBC News 'there are methods' for doing so," *NBC News*, March 30, 2025, https://www.nbcnews.com/politics /donald-trump/trump-third-term-white-house-methods-rcna198752.

161. *claim to be president*: The latter situation would, of course, engender separate litigation over whether that stratagem is precluded by the Twenty-Second Amendment.

161. *Brazil and France, respectively*: Kahn, "A Brazil Court"; Joseph Ataman et al., "Far-right leader Marine Le Pen banned from 2027 presidential race, throwing French politics into disarray," *CNN*, March 31, 2025, https://edition.cnn.com /2025/03/31/europe/marine-le-pen-embezzlement-trial-verdict-france-intl.

161. *in numerous US states*: Kahn, "A Brazil Court"; Gary Fields and Josh Funk, "State laws vary widely on whether felons can run for office," *AP News*, January 19, 2023, https://apnews.com/article/illinois-state-government-west-virginia-new -mexico-nebraska-legal-proceedings-a640fea829456d6cfb2c0d9e97a1dfa3.

162. *by the Constitution*: US Const. art. II, § 4; ibid., art. I, § 5.

162. *override the Constitution*: *Marbury v. Madison*, 5 U.S. (1 Cranch) 137, 180 (1803).

162. *Constitution is amended*: A similar issue would arise when a candidate for office lies but is then permitted to assume office before a debarment proceeding can be decided. In cases where the candidate loses, this is not a problem, as there is ample time to adjudicate the issue, as was the case with Bolsonaro. But a system for expedited review will be needed in cases where the candidate wins or else a debarment remedy will only be effective prospectively.

163. *chooses to lie*: One potential hurdle to a criminal prosecution is the statute of limitations. This problem is soluble. The statute of limitations is the time by which the government must charge a crime. Pursuant to a congressional statute, the general rule for federal crimes is that an indictment must be brought within five years of the crime occurring. But there are some crimes that have longer time frames, and there are ways to exclude time under that five-year clock. The statute of limitations problem arises when you have a politicized White House in control of the Department of Justice, and that administration (or the next one similarly politicized) is continuously in office for more than five years. Of course, there are both Republican and Democratic administrations that do not politicize the Department of Justice and routinely prosecute public corruption regardless of party. White House senior aide Scooter Libby was prosecuted under a Republican administration; the president's own son was prosecuted in a Democratic one. But a corrupted Department of Justice could run out the clock so that no indictment is brought within five years of the lie. The solution is to provide in the new model law that the statute of limitations is longer, say ten or twelve years, to reduce the risk of this occurring. Alternatively, the law could provide that the five-year statute is tolled — that is a legal term meaning the time clock is paused — until a change of party control of the executive branch.

163. *by the Supreme Court*: Kathryn Watson, "Can a president pardon himself?," *CBS News*, May 30, 2024, https://www.cbsnews.com/news/can-a-president -pardon-himself/.

163. *in his own case*: Mary C. Lawton, "Presidential or Legislative Pardon of the President," Office of Legal Counsel, August 5, 1974, https://www.justice.gov/file /147746/dl?inline.

163. *no obvious exception*: Jonathan Turley, "Yes, Donald Trump can pardon himself, but it would be a disastrous idea," *USA Today*, June 4, 2018, https://www.usatoday .com/story/opinion/2018/06/04/donald-trump-self-pardon-constitutional -impeachment-column/667751002/.

Conclusion

166. *against Holocaust denial*: Strafgesetzbuch [StGB], § 130(3) (Germany).

166. *barred Jair Bolsonaro*: Jack Nicas, "Brazil Bars Bolsonaro From Office for Election-Fraud Claims," *New York Times*, June 30, 2023, https://www.nytimes .com/2023/06/30/world/americas/bolsonaro-brazil-banned-office.html; Ana Ionova and Jack Nicas, "Bolsonaro Sentenced to 27 Years in Prison for Plotting Coup in Brazil," *New York Times*, September 11, 2025, https://www.nytimes .com/2025/09/11/world/americas/bolsonaro-convicted-coup-attempt.html.

166. *core societal bonds*: Lei Complementar No. 135, de 4 de Junho de 2010, art. 2 (Brazil); Code Pénal art. 131-26-1 (France).

166. *convicted of a crime*: "Restoration of Rights Project," Collateral Consequences Resource Center, https://ccresourcecenter.org/restoration-2-2/.

166. *a suicide pact*: Jacob Sullum, "'The Constitution Is Not a Suicide Pact,'" *Reason*, February 2025, https://reason.com/2025/01/11/not-a-suicide-pact/.

167. *a toxic stew*: This amalgam of forces confronting liberal democracies across the globe is cogently described in the work of da Empoli. In *L'heure des Predateurs*,

he depicts how these antidemocratic forces have outmaneuvered the coalition of institutionalists, human-rights defenders, and intellectuals who presumed the stability of liberal norms. In the face of this threat, he, too, calls for bold action by the forces for democracy.

167. *for a democracy*: *Youngstown Sheet & Tube Co. v. Sawyer*, 343 U.S. 579, 634 (1952) (Jackson, J., concurring in the judgment and opinion).

167. *effort in Korea*: Ibid., 583, 588–89 (Jackson, J., concurring in the judgment and opinion).

168. *first Nuremberg trial*: David Noonan, "At Nuremberg, World War II's Battle Turned to the Courtroom, and an Eloquent Lawyer Helped Lead the Allies to Victory," *Smithsonian Magazine*, November 2025, https://www.smithsonianmag .com/history/nuremburg-world-war-ii-battle-turned-courtroom-eloquent -lawyer-lead-allies-victory-180987465/.

168. *to be tried there*: Ibid.

168. *name of public safety*: Ibid., 651 (Jackson, J., concurring in the judgment and opinion).

168. *never to be restored*: Ibid. (Jackson, J., concurring in the judgment and opinion).

168. *to kindle emergencies*: Ibid., 650 (Jackson, J., concurring in the judgment and opinion).

169. *cancels their effectiveness*: Ibid., 653–54 (Jackson, J., concurring in the judgment and opinion). President Woodrow Wilson observed that the President's commands, as both a leader of a party and of a nation, can be "irresistible" (ibid., 654).

169. *fine people*: Glenn Thrush and Maggie Haberman, "Trump Gives White Supremacists an Unequivocal Boost," *New York Times*, August 15, 2017, https: //www.nytimes.com/2017/08/15/us/politics/trump-charlottesville-white -nationalists.html.

169. *America's Hitler*: Gram Slattery and Helen Coster, "JD Vance once compared Trump to Hitler. Now, he is Trump's vice president-elect," Reuters, November 6, 2024, https://www.reuters.com/world/us/jd-vance-once-compared-trump-hitler -now-they-are-running-mates-2024-07-15/.

170. *countless other proposals*: A thoughtful discussion of other ideas is contained in *After Trump*, written at the end of the first Trump Administration by two people at opposite ends of the political spectrum, but aligned in their love of country. See: Bob Bauer and Jack Goldsmith, *After Trump* (Washington, DC: Lawfare Institute, 2020).

172. *to pass away*: *Youngstown Sheet & Tube Co. v. Sawyer*, 343 U.S., 655 (Jackson, J., concurring in the judgment and opinion).

172. *to give them up*: Ibid. (Jackson, J., concurring in the judgment and opinion).

Acknowledgments

173. *true friends are*: Jack Smith, "The State of the United States: A Conversation with Jack Smith," moderated by Andrew Weissmann, October 14, 2025, University College London Faculty of Laws, *YouTube*, 1:17:15, https://www.youtube.com /watch?v=DR79GW6SvxE.

INDEX

Andrew Weissmann is an NYU Law School professor and widely respected legal analyst on MS NOW. He was a lead prosecutor in Robert S. Mueller's Special Counsel's Office, chief of the Fraud Section in the Department of Justice, general counsel of the Federal Bureau of Investigation under Director Mueller, a leader of the Enron Task Force, and an organized-crime prosecutor in Brooklyn. He is a co-host of MS NOW's award-winning podcast *Main Justice* and, before that, *Prosecuting Donald Trump*. He has written two *New York Times* bestsellers, *Where Law Ends: Inside the Mueller Investigation*, and, as co-author, *The Trump Indictments*, and also writes the widely followed Substack newsletter *Behind the Headlines*. Weissmann holds degrees from Princeton and Columbia Law School, was a Fulbright scholar, and teaches criminal procedure and national security law at NYU School of Law. Weissmann is a New Yorker through and through.